Clinical Co-Management

A Bridge to Clinical Integration and Pathway to Bundled Payments

Clinical Co-Management

A Bridge to Clinical Integration and Pathway to Bundled Payments

Cherilyn G. Murer, JD, CRA

Foreword by Mark D. Birdwhistell, University of Kentucky

CRC Press is an imprint of the
Taylor & Francis Group, an **informa** business
A PRODUCTIVITY PRESS BOOK

CRC Press
Taylor & Francis Group
6000 Broken Sound Parkway NW, Suite 300
Boca Raton, FL 33487-2742

Printed on acid-free paper
Version Date: 20150630

International Standard Book Number-13: 978-1-4987-0462-5 (Hardback)

Visit the Taylor & Francis Web site at
http://www.taylorandfrancis.com

and the CRC Press Web site at
http://www.crcpress.com

Contents

Foreword

I have worked in healthcare administration in both private and public sectors for more than three decades. In all of these capacities, I have been extensively involved in the policy and regulatory arenas. The current healthcare landscape is changing at a faster pace than I have experienced during the previous 30 years. Individuals who have not had healthcare coverage are acquiring coverage. At the same time, governmental and private payers are focusing on ways to decrease costs through reduced or alternative payment approaches to providers of care.

Healthcare providers are being challenged to supply more services with less revenue. This has become commonly referred to as the "more-for-less" phenomenon.

Among the many rapid changes in this national environment is the realization that disparate healthcare institutions that have never worked collaboratively are increasingly finding the need and reason to partner on the delivery of healthcare services. A primary method to reduce costs in a healthcare system involves aligning members' strengths with members' weaknesses.

The healthcare environment encompasses a host of political, social, cultural, and regulatory factors that must be bridged as healthcare institutions begin exploring partnership opportunities.

Developing these partnering opportunities into effective relationships requires a managerial framework that builds trust, provides incentives for quality outcomes, and aligns interests. This is particularly the case when bringing together providers and administrators from different types of healthcare organizations such as academic medical centers and community providers.

The University of Kentucky's medical center operates under the brand name of UK HealthCare.

A decade ago, UK HealthCare in its strategic plan recognized the need to reposition itself as a regional referral center, focusing on advanced subspecialty care for the entire state of Kentucky and its bordering counties. The goal was to become a "medical destination" for patients from that region who needed access to specialized care, allowing them to remain in the state.

To support that goal, UK HealthCare employed a regionalization approach, establishing a virtual network of partnering provider organizations throughout Kentucky and beyond. Embarking on that path, UK HealthCare assisted community providers in dealing with their challenges. By working together, UK HealthCare and its partners are giving Kentuckians access to the appropriate levels of care as close to home as possible.

Cherilyn Murer and her team of experts introduced UK HealthCare to the Clinical Co-Management Agreement (CCMA), a tool that has been an excellent way for UK HealthCare to engage with its partnering organizations. A CCMA gives physicians and administrators a voice and process for aligning their respective interests and expertise through a system of protocols, outcome targets, and quality metrics.

UK HealthCare's regionalization strategy has been enhanced by the use of the CCMA tool. This method has provided the structure and discipline necessary for different healthcare entities to establish trust, which is so essential to effectively partnering and improving the healthcare of Kentuckians in this new environment.

Mark D. Birdwhistell
Former Secretary of the Kentucky Cabinet for Health and Family Services
Frankfurt, Kentucky
Current Vice-President for Administration and External Affairs, UK HealthCare
Lexington, Kentucky

Acknowledgments

For over 20 years, I have had the pleasure of working with Kris Mednansky as a publisher and as a respected colleague. Kris is highly regarded in her field and has an uncanny understanding of the intricacies of the American healthcare delivery system. She gently nudges and prods to deadline, but with sensitivity to the many business commitments of her authors.

I am so very grateful to Kris for shepherding this book to publication, and I look forward to a long and continued collaboration.

This book is representative of the experiences of Murer Consultants in the field, working with extraordinary clients who are the leaders of our industry. As our firm celebrates a milestone 30th anniversary, I thank the individuals who have embraced the concept of Clinical Co-Management and have worked diligently through the process of formulating the new language of clinical integration. Special recognition must go to the financial and data analysts, the department chairs, and nurse managers, who understood the true essence of CCMA, which is based on the validation of data, to ensure the accuracy of baseline and target physician incentive metrics.

This book is also reflective of the collegial culture of Murer Consultants. My deepest thanks to Anthony DelRio, senior consultant, for his insights and vast knowledge and love of language. We would discuss, for hours, the selection of individual words to ensure we were conveying the most accurate interpretation of the Office of Inspector General (OIG) advisory opinions, which provided us with regulatory guidance for CCMA structuring.

Brian Sils, who will receive his master's degree in June from the University of Chicago Harris School of Public Policy, has brought a new dimension to the legal-based Murer Consultants. His expertise in data mining and analytics was the backbone of our research, in particular, related to the historical perspective and context from which CCMA has evolved. It was such a joy to work closely with Anthony and Brian, who believed in this project and encouraged its prioritization on days when the priorities were too numerous to count. Also, a special thank you to Ryan Bailey, the Murer senior consultant, who catalogued the metrics used in developing CCMA for clients.

It would be a glaring omission to write a book on physician/hospital integration without a physician's perspective. Dr. Sasha Demos brought a fresh dimension to the inherent issues and concerns of practicing physicians. Sasha is a scientist, who in addition to her medical degree from the University of Chicago holds a PhD in bioengineering. She also has an appreciation for the complexities of administration, serving as the chair of the Department of Anesthesiology at Edward Hospital, a large tertiary community hospital in Chicago's western suburbs. She is also my daughter, so my appreciation for her contributions to this book is sprinkled with great pride.

And to my partners, Michael Murer and Lyndean Brick, I would like to express my deepest appreciation for their support, counsel, and ever-present encouragement.

A firm is built on the foundation of its principles. This triad has anchored Murer Consultants for almost three decades, weathering storms and basking in the warmth of creativity by providing pragmatic solutions to the daily challenges faced by our evolving healthcare industry.

Cherilyn G. Murer, JD, CRA

Author

Cherilyn G. Murer, JD, CRA, founder, president, and CEO of Murer Consultants, Mokena, Illinois, has long been an active voice in the advancement of quality, cost-effective healthcare. Ms. Murer received a Juris Doctor degree with honors from Northern Illinois University and has coupled her background in law with her previous operational experience as the director of Rehabilitation Medicine at Northwestern Memorial Hospital, Chicago, Illinois. Dr. Murer is a sought-after lecturer and educator whose focus is on assisting her clients in navigating through the complex regulatory, strategic, and financial issues facing healthcare today. With a national client base, Murer Consultants represents large multi-hospital healthcare systems, academic medical centers, and large physician group practices focusing on strategic positioning, consolidation and acquisition, regulatory compliance, and financial management.

In her role as president and CEO of Murer Consultants, Dr. Murer has been instrumental in the development and implementation of Clinical Co-Management as a tool to align stakeholders' interests in the healthcare field. She has shown time and again the value of Clinical Co-Management nationwide in settings ranging from academic medical centers to large hospital systems. As a recognized innovator in payment delivery mechanisms, Dr. Murer has demonstrated the viability of Clinical Co-Management as a delivery system moving forward with health reform.

In keeping with her commitment to policy and health reform, Dr. Murer was appointed to the University of Chicago Harris School of Public Policy, Dean's International Council. This prestigious group serves as advisors to the Harris School regarding the issues of international importance and new policy initiatives.

In May 2005, Dr. Murer received a gubernatorial appointment, with senate confirmation, to a six-year term to the Northern Illinois University Board of Trustees. During this term, Dr. Murer has served as chairman of the board of this public university. In January 2011, Illinois Governor Pat Quinn reappointed Dr. Murer to the Northern Illinois University (NIU) Board of Trustees for another six-year term, and in September 2011, Dr. Murer was once again elected as chairman of the Board of Trustees. She and her husband, Michael, have provided a philanthropic gift to NIU to establish the "Murer Initiative" as a forum for scholarly discussion, policy analysis, and cross-disciplinary integration of medicine, law, technology, and finance. In 2002, Dr. Murer was appointed to the Northern Illinois University Law School's prestigious Board of Visitors and was honored with its 2003 College of Law Distinguished Alumni Award. In 2014, she accepted a two-year term on the Board of Directors of Solve the Organ Shortage (SOS), an international effort to end the organ shortage through science, partnership, and policy. Also, in 2014, she was appointed to the Advisory Council of the Buck Institute for Research on Aging, a research facility focused solely on understanding the connection between aging and chronic disease.

Since 2003, Dr. Murer has held an appointment to the faculty of the University of Illinois at Chicago College of Medicine as a clinical assistant professor of law in the Department of Family Medicine. She conducts Grand Rounds Lectures targeted to both the faculty practice and residents, orienting them to healthcare trends and key issues impacting the practice of family practice in today's changing environment.

Coinciding with the firm's 25th anniversary, Dr. Murer was honored by both the University of Illinois at Chicago and Northern Illinois University. In February 2010, she was inducted into the prestigious Chicago Area Entrepreneurship Hall of Fame. In April, she received the 2010 Northern Illinois University Distinguished Alumni of the Year Award, the highest award given by the NIU Alumni Association to one individual each year who has achieved national, regional, or statewide prominence. In September 2011, she received the Lewis University Distinguished Alumni Award in recognition of her professional achievements. She subsequently accepted an invitation to serve on the Board of Trustees of this 8000 student LaSallian private university. Today, with growing enrollment, outstanding programs, experienced faculty, and motivated students, Lewis University is recognized as one of the finest, mid-sized, comprehensive Catholic universities in the country.

Dr. Murer has coauthored with Lyndean Lenhoff Brick and Michael A. Murer four books published by McGraw-Hill. *The Case Management Sourcebook*, a 300-page text, serves as a guide to designing and implementing a centralized case management system. A second book, published by McGraw-Hill and copublished by HFMA, entitled *Post Acute Care Reimbursement Manual: A Financial and Legal Guide*, addressed the financial impact on post-acute venues pre- and post-Balanced Budget Act of 1997 (BBA). A third book, *Compliance Audits and Plans for Healthcare*, was one of the first books to address complex healthcare compliance issues. A fourth book, *Medical Records Management*, is an 800-page complete guide to disclosure, retention, and technology. A fifth book was published in April 2003 by Commerce Clearing House, Inc. (CCH), entitled *Understanding Provider-Based Status*. A sixth book, *The Case Management Workbook: A Road Map to an Effective Integrated Health System*, published through CRC Press (a Routledge-Taylor & Francis Group) was released on March 22, 2011.

Chapter 1

Defining Clinical Co-Management and Its Impact on Effective and Efficient Healthcare Delivery

Why Clinical Co-Management?

The American healthcare system is a complex integration of medical, social, economic, technological, legal, and governmental issues. Understanding the healthcare system requires more than looking at each issue as an individual silo, in isolation from the rest. It requires seeing the system holistically, understanding how the parts interconnect and interact with one another, and realizing that a number of underlying cultural, political, and social mores inform and affect the system. The problem that the healthcare system faces today is essentially the same problem it has faced for decades: alignment. Lacking alignment of incentives and accountability has had a dramatic impact, distorting the growth of medical costs while diverting focus from delivering efficient, high-quality care. There has always been active discussion, among many sectors, of accountability in healthcare and the need for aligning the multitude of interests involved. But the financial, political, and structural pressure necessary to move from talk to action has been largely absent until recently. With the move away from volume payments to bundling that is on the horizon, the need for alignment and for the integration of clinical services has never been higher. The time is right to move to an integrated model.

Clinical Co-Management Is the Strategic and Regulatory Mechanism That Can Serve as the Catalyst in Truly Integrating a Healthcare System

Before moving forward, it is important to understand the path that brought us to where we are today. An entire chapter will be devoted to the historical perspective, but a brief overview is necessary to understand both the need for Clinical Co-Management and the problems that it seeks to address. That problem is, essentially, the prospective payment system (PPS). Originally passed as part of Social Security Amendments of 1983, PPS was a well-intentioned response to cost reimbursement, the system in which Medicare used to reimburse hospitals since the program's inception in 1965. From that point in 1965 through the Amendments in 1983, Medicare made payments to providers based upon the cost of services rendered and would pay whatever the provider reported on their cost report, within allowable parameters. As a fee-for-service arrangement and due to the fact that there was little oversight or uniformity in determining the prices being charged to Medicare, costs rose precipitously. In a 16-year period, from 1967 to 1983, Medicare payments to hospitals rose from $3 billion to $37 billion a year (United States Government, 2001, p. 1). PPS was the proposed solution to this with the government now paying a set amount for each procedure based upon diagnosis-related groups (DRGs) and modified slightly for geodemographic allowances. However, PPS was another pay for volume system and did little to slow the increasing growth rate of costs, which has ballooned to nearly $575 billion annually in 2012 (United States Government, 2013, p. 10).

The Problem, Again, Is Alignment

Under the PPS, hospital compensation was affected with more uniform reimbursement on a national basis; however, the reformed prospective payment system in no way addressed the alignment of physician incentive and practice behaviors. More recently, the government has unsuccessfully attempted to address the misalignment created by compensating volume while being concerned about quality and outcome. These attempts have focused primarily on hospitals, leaving physicians out of the equation. The lack of integration between physician and hospital incentives has only served to exacerbate the predicament. Recognizing this inherent misalignment, providers and policy makers have worked together to create an improved incentive paradigm. From those efforts, new and innovative methods of alignment and integration have begun to develop, but given the complex nature of the healthcare system, most providers are wary and cautious of implementing these new ideas.

To this end, a new division within the Centers for Medicare & Medicaid Services (CMS) was created to encourage pilot projects and nontraditional solutions to long-standing problems. The Center for Medicare and Medicaid Innovation (CMI) was first established by the Social Security Amendments of 1965 (Pub. L. 89–97, § 1115) and expanded under the Affordable Care Act (Pub. L. 111–148, § 3021). These centers were created to test new and innovative payment and delivery models that enhance quality while reducing expenditures. The Innovation Center engages a wide range of stakeholders as it develops these models and then selects organizations through competitive processes to test them in clinical settings. Evaluations are then completed to analyze the quality of care and spending changes under the new payment and delivery methods. The lessons and best practices garnered from these tests are then disseminated to improve both CMS and the wider healthcare system. The Innovation Center focuses its efforts on the following categories: incentivizing accountable care, offering bundled payments, strengthening primary care, focusing on jointly funded Medicaid and Children's Health Insurance Program (CHIP) programs, supporting dual eligible Medicare and Medicaid enrollees, speeding the adoption of best practices, and accelerating the development of new payment and delivery models (Centers for Medicare & Medicaid Services, p. 1).

What Is Clinical Co-Management?

One of the most promising innovations and opportunities for goal alignment in the health system today is Clinical Co-Management. In its broadest sense, Clinical Co-Management is a step on the path toward fully integrated healthcare. As healthcare-related costs continue to rise and reimbursements continue to decline, gains in efficiency must be made in order to keep both hospitals and physicians competitive. Clinical Co-Management serves as the catalyst to an effective integration process, creating the framework through which the delivery, management, and organization of healthcare services can be coordinated among hospitals and physicians and through which those gains in efficiency can be realized. Clinical Co-Management also represents a real opportunity for hospitals and physicians to lead quality improvement and cost-containment efforts. As such, these efforts can be based upon quality of care if led by hospitals and physicians instead of by payers, which has been the case traditionally.

More specifically, Clinical Co-Management is a means for the hospital and its medical staff to share the responsibility of both the administrative and clinical oversight of either a particular service line or an entire facility. With this increased share of responsibility comes some amount of increased risk assumed by the physicians, risk that is offset by a system of rewards. And in compensation for this assumed risk, hospitals and physicians enter into a Clinical Co-Management Agreement (CCMA) whereby hospitals provide physicians financial incentives for improving their performance. A CCMA is the legal mechanism that defines and describes the collaborative relationship that hospitals and physicians enter into. It also provides a legal structure through which hospitals and physicians can align their respective philosophies, visions, practices, and financial interests. It takes more than a legal mechanism or a legal structure to improve the system though.

Failure Lies in a Silo Perspective

In isolation, CCMAs cannot function. For some time, lawmakers have had a vision of bundling healthcare services and of the cost savings that would be generated. While it is true that laws often follow this vision and this intent, sometimes the policies in place limp behind, creating an environment where implementation is untenable. Until recently, this was the case with CCMAs where laws have limped behind vision and implementation has lagged behind intent. Several existing laws related to fraud and abuse (the Anti-Kickback Statute, the Ethics in Patient Referrals Act also known as the Stark Law, and the Civil Monetary Penalty Law) have created roadblocks to CCMAs that were not originally intended nor can be readily overcome, hence the limp in the process. These laws will be introduced later in this chapter and will have an entire chapter dedicated to them later in the book. When forging ahead with CCMAs though, especially with laws that make it difficult to translate the best of intentions and the boldest of visions into reality, we must proceed judiciously. Fortunately, the Office of Inspector General (OIG) has been able to alleviate that limp somewhat with guidance regarding CCMAs in 2008 and 2012 with Advisory Opinions 08–16 and 12–22, respectively, which have given guidance on acceptable practices. This kind of leadership is critical going forward to further clarify the legal landscape and to facilitate further integration and alignment of clinical practice and monetary interests.

CCMAs can be powerful tools to drive this alignment. This is due in part to the role that physicians play within a CCMA and the incentives they receive as a result. First, CCMAs allow physicians the freedom and autonomy to manage a particular line of service, a specific location, or an entire hospital. Second, the financial benefits physicians receive incentivize them to become active partners in regard to improving quality, efficiency, and satisfaction across areas of need as identified by the hospital. To accomplish this, under a CCMA, physicians are paid a base fee plus some bonus compensation for satisfying certain quality, operational efficiency, patient and/or staff satisfaction, and program development benchmarks. In essence, CCMAs are a mechanism through which physicians are provided a fair market value payment for advancing both high-quality and cost-efficient care. CCMAs may also include other efficiency measures, whereby physicians share in the differential of costs saved over a period of time. There are legal considerations to take into account regarding some of these arrangements and those considerations will be explored in depth in subsequent chapters.

Clinical Co-Management is becoming an increasingly popular model to integrate and coordinate healthcare activities. Not only does the coordination between hospitals and physicians lead to reduced costs, increased quality of care, and improved satisfaction, but also it allows physicians, within a hospital, to have a voice in decision making and to become active participants in implementing meaningful improvements. Historically, hospitals and physicians have not effectively partnered in the planning, the management, nor the oversight of their respective service lines and as a result, quality and efficiency have suffered while costs have increased unabated. Other models have tried to improve this coordination problem in the past, namely that of medical director arrangements. Due to the limited number of physicians actually involved in this process, buy-in among the broader group of physicians has been low and the general focus has remained on quantity, not quality of care. The concept of Clinical Co-Management is not new in and of itself, but interest in the model has grown since healthcare reform and since CMS proposed regulatory changes in 2008 that would make CCMAs more feasible and attractive. As it is now though, CCMAs are still relatively new and will certainly continue to evolve as more programs are continually being developed and implemented.

Benefits of Clinical Co-Management

As mentioned previously, the most important benefits that a CCMA can offer are the improvements in quality and efficiency, the proactive and accountable participation of physicians in operations and service-line management, and the alignment of hospital and physician incentives. CCMA arrangements present a viable alternative to conventional alignment models, including medical directorships, committee chairs, and physician employment, which have traditionally failed to maximize quality and efficiency. This is due in part to the pluralistic approach to performance taken by CCMAs. They engage the services of potentially all participating physicians to oversee the day-to-day performance of the service line in contrast to conventional models that only engage small numbers of physicians. Figure 1.1 illustrates this point. As physician engagement increases throughout the models, responsibilities and risks increase, but so do the benefits to all parties involved.

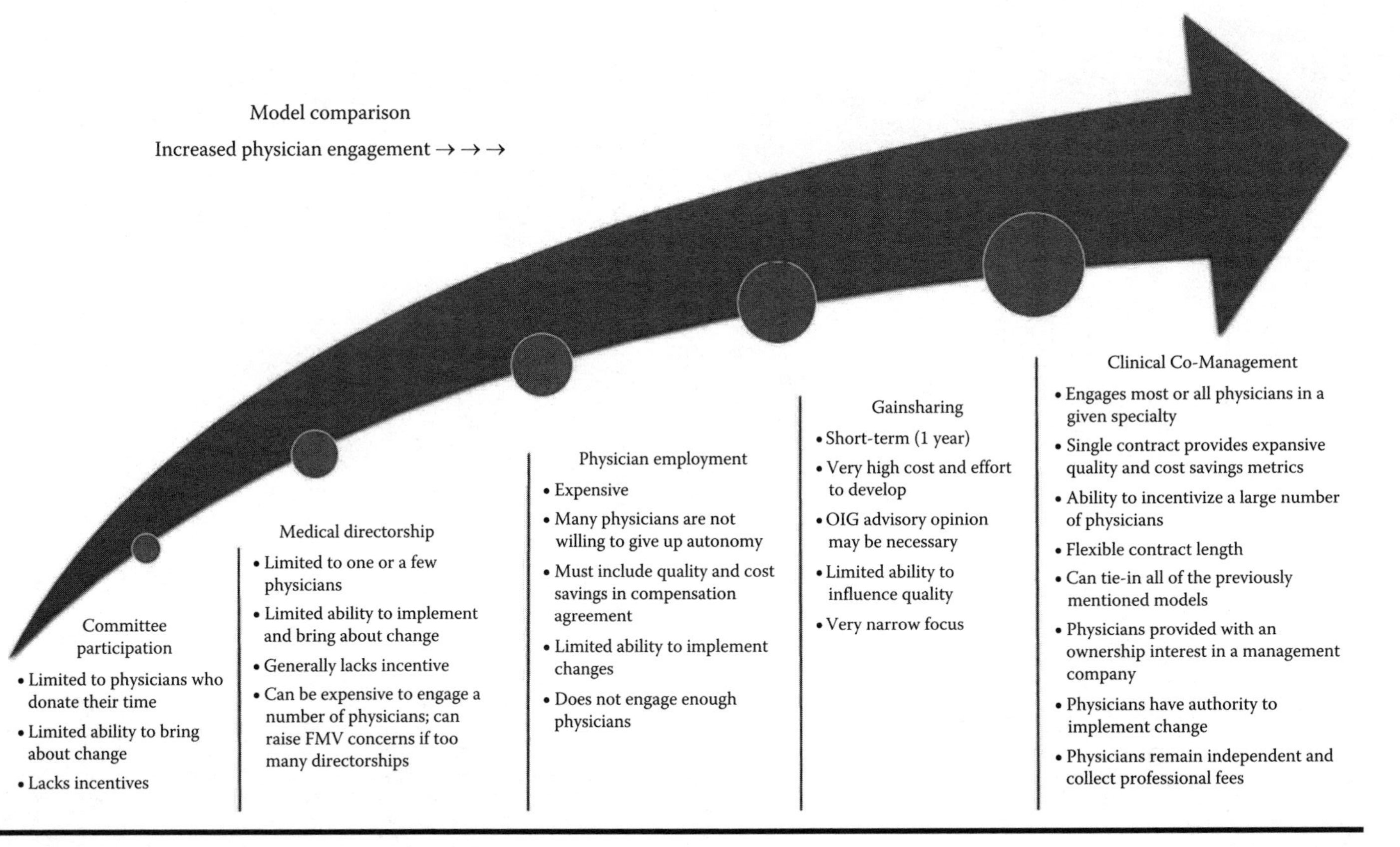

Figure 1.1 Physician engagement model.

Another critical benefit of CCMAs in regard to physician autonomy is the ability to continue collecting professional fee payments from their practice without any changes brought about from the CCMA. Physician engagement along with physician independence, combined with physicians having ownership and managerial interests along with the actual authority to implement change, leads to both wider buy-in among physicians and to the improvements in healthcare delivery quality and efficiency. This is a departure from historical management contracts, which are often with nonphysicians. CCMAs allow physicians that are involved in a particular line of service to manage its outcomes and efficiency, thereby placing greater responsibility in the hands of the clinical experts that direct the care of the hospital's patients.

CCMAs can also effectively resolve some of the inefficiencies that are inherent to many traditional medical staff structures. In these, physicians must volunteer their time to participate in quality committee meetings and other mechanisms that are used to improve both service line and hospital performance. Due to constraints on time and financial considerations though, physicians cannot continually follow up and remain engaged in this process without some type of incentive. CCMAs can provide physicians with reimbursement for services to committees as well as for time spent working on the identified issues after such meetings. Likewise, CCMAs incentivize physicians to become more engaged in this oversight process because there are financial rewards at stake. This directly translates to an inherent sense of ownership over the service line's performance, which is currently not present under existing models. Without the input and without the enthusiasm of the physicians who are responsible for the care of the service-line patients, other models will continue to result in subpar performance in the areas of quality, efficiency, and satisfaction, which will in turn result in lost revenue for the hospital and physicians alike.

CCMA Development Process

Although the CCMA development process will be covered in more depth over the course of Chapter 6, it is important to give a brief overview to aid in the understanding of what CCMAs are and how to successfully create one. The first step in the process is the formation of a steering committee that represents both the hospital and the medical staff. It is important at this stage that both parties clearly articulate goals and desires and that a consensus is achieved in regard to philosophy, vision, and conflict resolution. The steering committee is also tasked with developing a plan of action which includes the following:

1. Determining the scope of the CCMA
2. Identifying areas of need using hospital data
3. Developing quality, operational efficiency, and satisfaction metrics using historical baseline data
4. Developing a list of base co-management services and duties

Figure 1.2 illustrates some potential services that could be included as part of a CCMA. Table 1.1 illustrates a sample metric with desired improvement, the baseline number from the hospital, a national benchmark, and a tiered structure to which levels of payout are tied.

After the scope, metrics, and duties have been agreed upon, the next step in development is to determine physician compensation structure. As mentioned previously, compensation is broken up into a base fee in addition to some amount of incentive pay. Incentive compensation can be arranged in several different ways. Incentive measures can be based on some amount of improvement regarding a particular metric, or it can be based on achieving certain agreed upon targets. Incentive measures may also be progressive, paying out different amounts for reaching certain quality levels, or they can

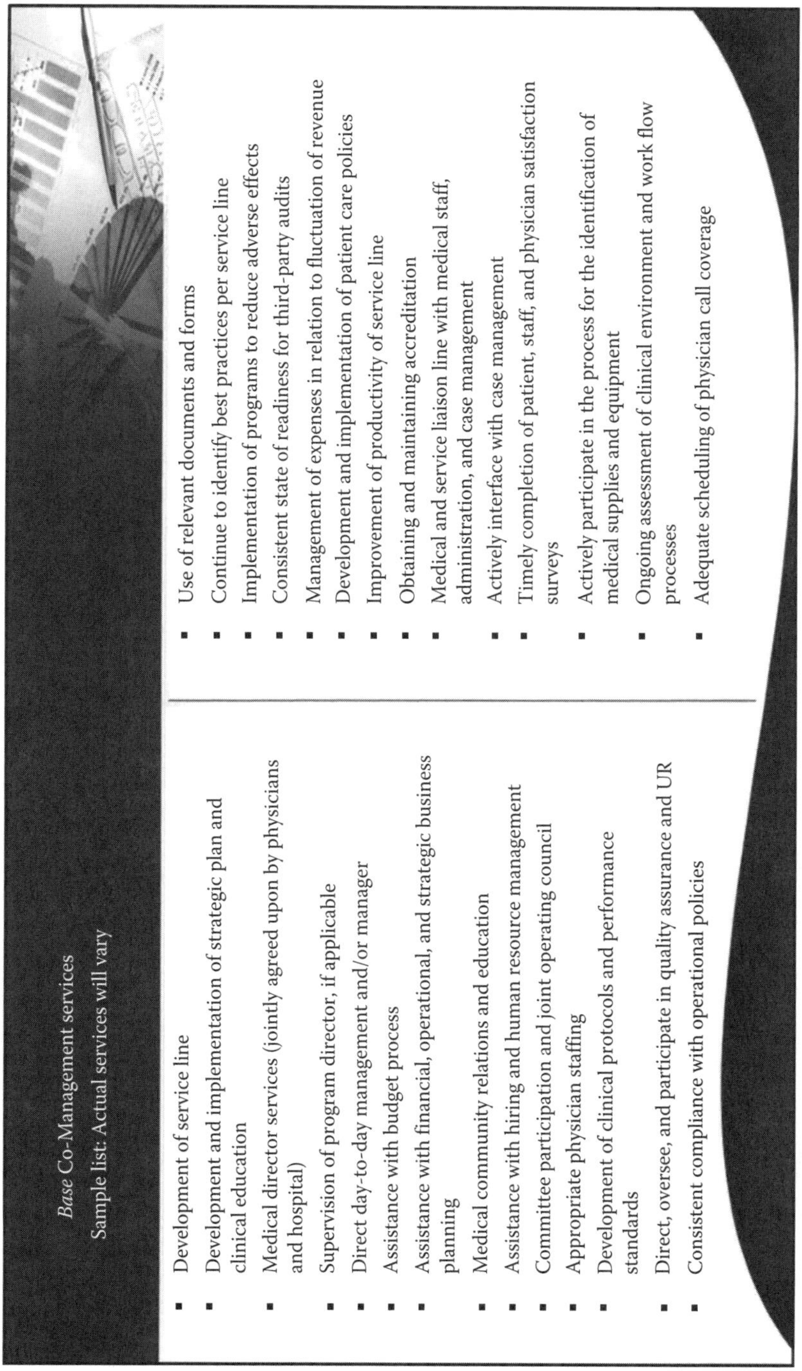

Base Co-Management services

Sample list: Actual services will vary

- Development of service line
- Development and implementation of strategic plan and clinical education
- Medical director services (jointly agreed upon by physicians and hospital)
- Supervision of program director, if applicable
- Direct day-to-day management and/or manager
- Assistance with budget process
- Assistance with financial, operational, and strategic business planning
- Medical community relations and education
- Assistance with hiring and human resource management
- Committee participation and joint operating council
- Appropriate physician staffing
- Development of clinical protocols and performance standards
- Direct, oversee, and participate in quality assurance and UR
- Consistent compliance with operational policies
- Use of relevant documents and forms
- Continue to identify best practices per service line
- Implementation of programs to reduce adverse effects
- Consistent state of readiness for third-party audits
- Management of expenses in relation to fluctuation of revenue
- Development and implementation of patient care policies
- Improvement of productivity of service line
- Obtaining and maintaining accreditation
- Medical and service liaison line with medical staff, administration, and case management
- Actively interface with case management
- Timely completion of patient, staff, and physician satisfaction surveys
- Actively participate in the process for the identification of medical supplies and equipment
- Ongoing assessment of clinical environment and work flow processes
- Adequate scheduling of physician call coverage

Figure 1.2 Potential CCMA base services.

Table 1.1 Sample Metric

Metric	*Improvement*	*Baseline (%)*	*Benchmark (%)*	*Tiered Structure (%)*	*% Payout*
Hospital 30-day same or similar diagnosis risk standardized readmission rate (RSRR) following heart failure (HF) hospitalization	Decrease in rate	29	23	≥29	0
				29–27	25
				27–25	50
				25–23	75
				≤23	100

be an all-or-nothing type of arrangement. Regardless of the system, incentives should be based upon objective, verifiable, measureable, and medically credible metrics. It is also crucial that fair market value be utilized in determining compensation, which is determined based upon the services and fees offered. Once this has been accomplished, a management company is formed. These can also take a number of forms with physicians contracting directly with hospitals, forming an LLC, or having a joint venture with the hospital. Management duties can then include the following:

1. Patient care management
2. Quality
3. Administrative management
4. Patient, employee, and physician satisfaction
5. Supply and service management
6. Financial management
7. Personnel
8. Marketing

Once all of these steps have been completed, the CCMA can be executed and the program can be rolled out. Figure 1.3 illustrates how a sample CCMA model functions.

One of the unintended and most significant benefits to this type of developmental process is the validation of hospital data. An arrangement like a CCMA makes this process critical and places a spotlight on the timeliness, accuracy, and completeness of data. If the data collected by the hospital are incomplete or errant in some way the baseline data will be skewed. If the baseline data are skewed, then targeted quality improvements will likewise be incorrect. If the reported baseline for a metric is 13% but in reality is actually 11%, hospitals may be required to compensate physicians for doing nothing to improve care. Conversely, if the reported baseline is 13% but in reality is 22%, it will be incredibly difficult to reach targeted improvements no matter how much effort is

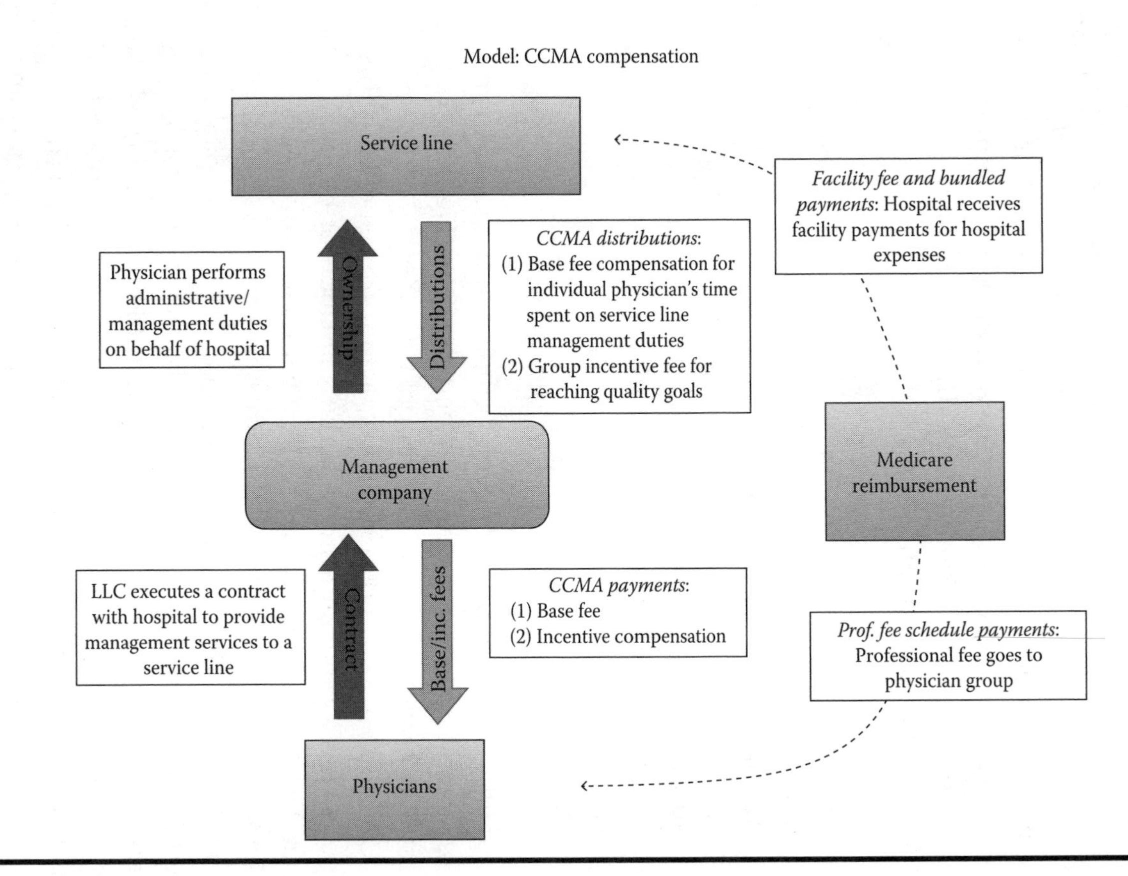

Figure 1.3 Sample CCMA structure.

exerted by both parties. In this regard, compensation to physicians will not be commensurate with improvements in quality. This developmental process allows hospitals and physicians to engage in a back and forth to compare their own expectations with the data that are presented by the other party. It also serves as the beginning point of an iterative process that allows both parties to critically evaluate how they collect their data and what the true baseline values should be for their metrics.

Barriers to Successful Implementation

Like the CCMA development process, barriers to successful implementation will be expanded upon in the chapter on regulatory processes. But again, an overview at this point is important to introduce the three main areas of concern. They are as follows: the Anti-Kickback Statute (42 U.S.C. § 1320a-7b(b); 42 C.F.R. § 1001.952 et seq.), the Ethics in Patient Referrals Act (or the Stark Law) (42 U.S.C. § 1395nn et seq.; 42 C.F.R. § 411.350 et seq.), and the Civil Monetary Penalty Law (42 U.S.C. § 1320a-7(b) (1)-(2); 42 C.F.R. § 1003.100 et seq.). Tables 1.2 through 1.4 introduce each and describe how they are barriers to CCMA formation (Vasquez, 2011, pp. 4–6).

What to Expect?

Going forward, continued clinical integration will help to build stronger bonds between hospitals and physicians and yield increased quality of care provided at reduced costs. Healthcare delivery systems are continually increasing in complexity with Accountable Care Organizations (ACOs), bundled payment, and pay for performance becoming more prevalent. At this time, many hospital and physician groups are ill-prepared to adopt these more integrated models and will face significant

Table 1.2 Anti-Kickback Statute Summary

Law: Illegal to offer, pay, solicit, or receive any remuneration to induce or reward referrals of items or services reimbursable in whole or in part by federal or state healthcare programs.
General application: A hospital cannot provide a physician with anything of value (e.g. money, supplies, space) in exchange for the physician agreeing to refer patients to Hospital A.
CCMA application: Base and incentive fees tied to CCMAs, if structured incorrectly, could potentially appear to be a mechanism to pay for referrals, which would implicate Anti-Kickback Law.
Liability: Safe harbors, if met, can protect against criminal and civil liability. Potentially applicable safe harbors include personal services/management contracts and bona fide employment. Failure to meet a safe harbor does not, however, necessarily implicate liability.

Table 1.3 Stark Law Summary

Law: Stark Law prohibits physician referrals of designated health services for Medicare and Medicaid patients if the physician (or an immediate family member) has a financial relationship with that entity to which services are being referred.
General application: In the absence of an applicable Stark exception, a physician cannot refer a patient to a hospital if the physician has a financial relationship with the hospital.
CCMA application: Base and incentive fees under a CCMA create a financial relationship between the physician and the hospital. Due to the financial relationship, in the absence of an applicable Stark exception, physicians that a party to the CCMA cannot refer patients to the hospital.
Liability: The Stark Law is a strict liability statute (intent does not matter) that results in liability if a physician fails to meet an exception. Potential Stark exceptions include bona fide employment, fair market value, and personal services/management contract.

Table 1.4 Civil Monetary Penalty Law Summary

Law: Prohibits arrangements that, directly or indirectly, provide physicians with incentives to reduce or limit items or services to patients that are under clinical care.
General application: A hospital cannot give a physician anything of value in exchange for the physician reducing the amount of care provided to a patient.
CCMA application: Some CCMAs provide compensation to physicians in exchange for reducing costs in specific areas (e.g. use of supplies, implants, equipment, drugs).
Liability: There are no bright light exceptions or safe harbors under the Civil Monetary Penalty Law, which increases both uncertainty and risk for arrangements like CCMAs. However, the Health and Human Services Office of Inspector General has recognized safeguards in published advisory opinions.

challenges as healthcare delivery evolves. The integration, alignment, and engagement of physicians are critically imperative for organizations seeking to create high-performing, future-ready organizations. As physicians are likely to see continued reimbursement cuts though, they will be less likely to volunteer time for these activities. CCMAs are well suited to establish effective collaborations in the face of these difficulties though, being diverse and tailored toward specific needs instead of being rigid, one size fits all agreements.

This book seeks to discuss Clinical Co-Management from a number of perspectives in hopes that the information presented will be useful not only in understanding Clinical Co-Management as a concept, but in the actual development and implementation of CCMAs in real-world practices. Chapter 2 explores Clinical Co-Management from the historical perspective and provides a background of what has brought us to this point. Chapter 3 provides a prospective view of the role CCMAs will play as a bridge to bundled payments. Chapter 4 provides the physicians' perspective, going through unique challenges faced on a daily basis by a physician and how implementing CCMAs could benefit each individual stakeholder. Chapter 5 provides a regulatory analysis of the legal considerations that go into establishing a CCMA. Chapter 6 delves into Clinical Co-Management implementation, including the opportunities and difficulties associated with rollout. Chapter 7 provides a case study and a crash course on benchmarking and gives practical advice on both establishing and using performance metrics to improve quality and efficiency. And lastly, the conclusion provides insight as to the next steps in the Clinical Co-Management process and gives a glimpse into the future to see how Clinical Co-Management and healthcare can grow and open a world of new opportunities.

References

Brandt, A. S., Safriet, S. M., Hutzler, A., and Obletz, K. *Co-Management Arrangements: Common Issues with Development, Implementation and Valuation.* HealthCare Appraisers, Inc., 2011.

Centers for Medicare & Medicaid Services. About the CMS Innovation Center. innovation.cms.gov.

Mayes, R. The origins, development, and passage of Medicare's revolutionary prospective payment system. *Journal of the History of Medicine and Allied Sciences* 62(1):21–55 (2006).

United States Government. Office of Inspector General. *Medicare Hospital Prospective Payment System: How DRG Rates Are Calculated and Updated.* OEI-09-00-00200, August 2001.

United States Government. Boards of Trustees of the Federal Hospital Insurance and Federal Supplementary Medical Insurance Trust Funds. *2013 Annual Report of the Boards of Trustees of the Federal Hospital Insurance and Federal Supplementary Medical Insurance Trust Funds*, May 31, 2013.

Vasquez, K. and Van Leer, J. Co-managing your way to optimal quality and efficiency—A guide to clinical co-management agreements. *Annals of Health Law: Informed Consent.* Beazley Institute for Health Law and Policy, Chicago, 1.1, 2011.

Chapter 2

Clinical Co-Management in Historical Perspective

Introduction

Since the onset of Medicare in 1965, there has been an almost continuous call and need for reform. Payments from the federal government to providers grew at alarming rates from the very beginning and have contributed to an unsustainable growth rate in the healthcare market since that time. Today, we as a country are in a precarious situation. Health expenditures account for nearly 18% of our gross domestic product (GDP) (Figure 2.1), a number that far outpaces other countries. Additionally, Medicare costs have reached $575 billion annually (Figure 2.2). While Medicare's growth rate has recently slowed, aging demographics combined with increased chronic conditions along with a new class of eligible individuals as part of the Affordable Care Act make the future costs and solvency of Medicare and Medicaid a continued concern. There have been attempts to reform and reign in Medicare over the course of its history, but these have been reactionary in nature, going from one crisis to the next without any apparent long-term coherent structure. And due to the rapid nature

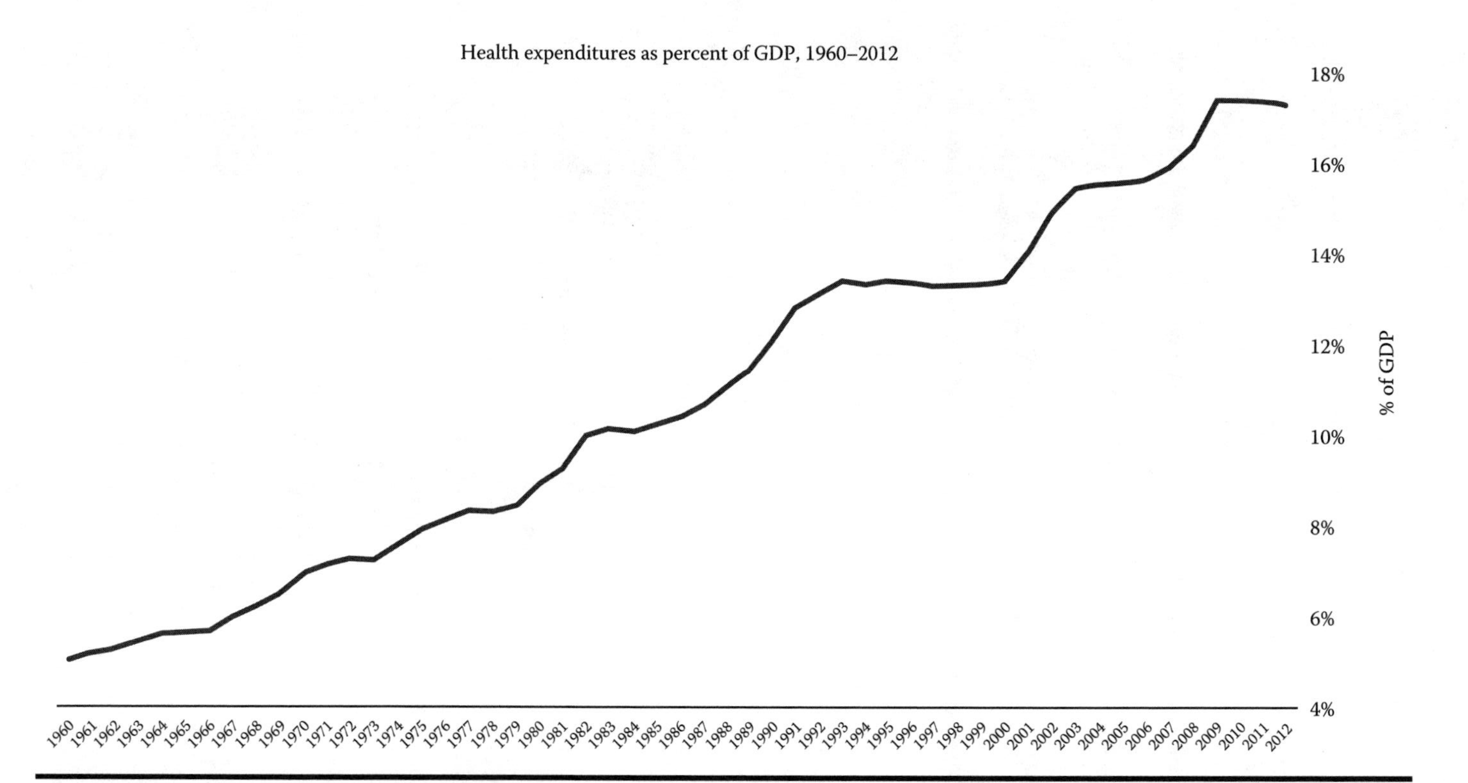

Figure 2.1 Growth of health expenditures as % of GDP. (From Centers for Medicare & Medicaid Services, National Health Expenditure Accounts, National health expenditures by type of service and source of funds, CY 1960–2012, Woodlawn, MD, January 7, 2014.)

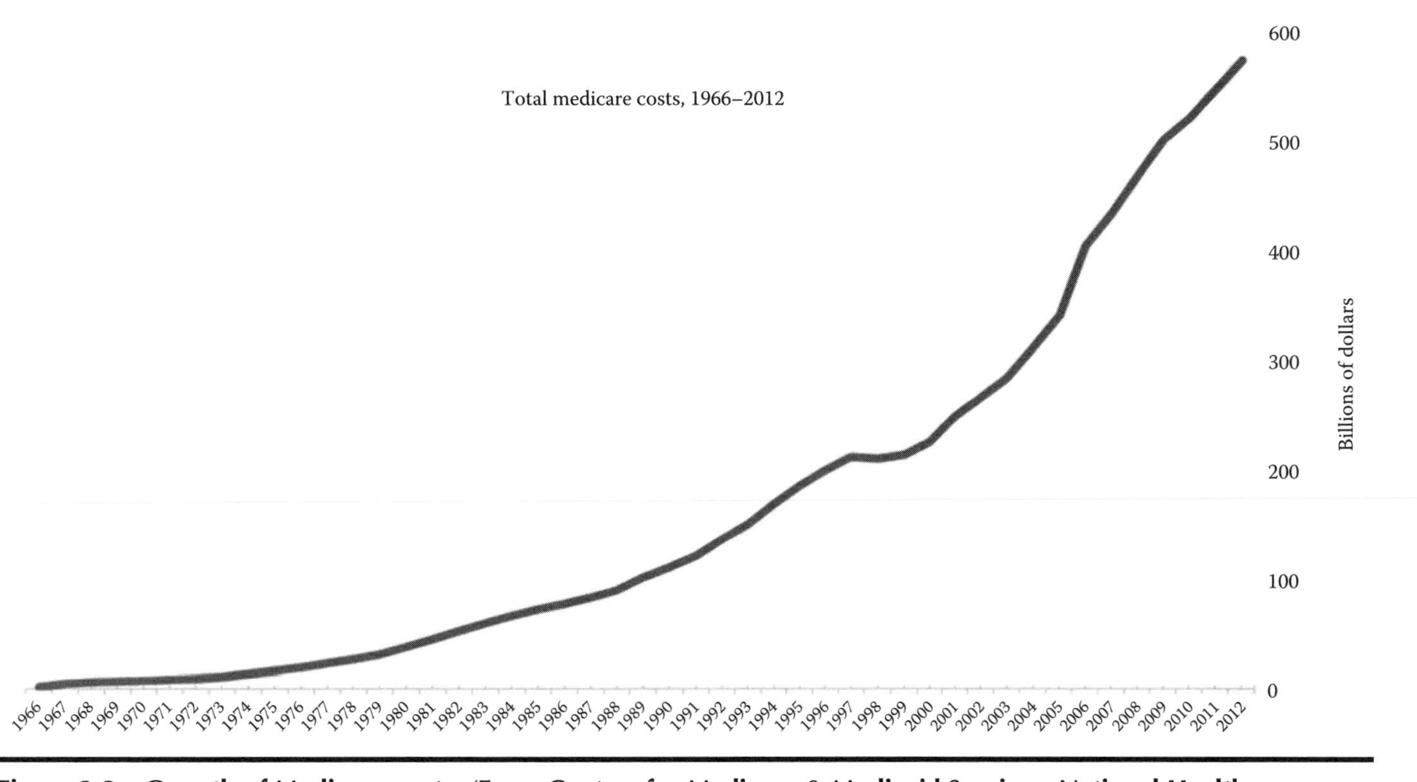

Figure 2.2 Growth of Medicare costs. (From Centers for Medicare & Medicaid Services, National Health Expenditure Accounts, National health expenditures by type of service and source of funds, CY 1960–2012, Woodlawn, MD, January 7, 2014.)

in which Medicare grew, the federal government has become a major player in the healthcare market, where its decisions have far-reaching consequences. As we shall see, the development and the subsequent singular reform focus on cost containment have created a system with perverse incentives, not only for Medicare but for the healthcare system at large. The focus has not been on how best to utilize scarce medical resources, what the real value of a procedure or medication might be, or how to best maximize the quality of care given the constraints of the system, rather hospitals and physicians have historically been paid to do more, regardless of the effectiveness, the costs, or the quality of care delivered. As such, there is a real need for a new payment and delivery paradigm that, while sensitive to current system, can begin to change the historical incentive and cost structure that has been at the root of the problem for so long.

Chapter 1 identified the biggest drivers toward CCMAs as rising healthcare costs and the misalignment of incentives between compensation, quality, and efficiency. Not coincidentally, these are the same problems that have plagued the wider healthcare system for decades. The reasons for this are many, including but not limited to the following:

- A lack of coordination and management as a result of a fragmented delivery system has led to inefficiencies and has driven up costs.
- Providers have had incentives to deliver more care, regardless of need or effectiveness, which has led to overutilization.
- The aging demographics of the patient population in combination with increased chronic conditions have also contributed to increased utilization.
- The number of patients insured and the intensity of care received have increased over time.
- Improvements and increased usage of medical technology have driven up the price of medical care.

- Lack of evidence as it pertains to effectiveness and value has impeded the adoption of the most efficient care.
- Patient demand and engagement with their care have also contributed to overutilization.

Understanding the history of the United States healthcare system, at least from 1965 when the government became a major player with the rollout of Medicare and Medicaid, is crucial to understanding the current environment and to planning where we should go in the future. We will focus on three periods in this chapter: Medicare's inception in 1965 to the introduction of the Prospective Payment System (PPS) in 1983, the effect of the PPS and the rise of managed care, and finally, the current environment including barriers and opportunities to moving forward with CCMAs. Additionally, within these periods, there exist a number of watershed years including 1965, 1983, 1997, and 2010. At each of these moments, healthcare delivery was fundamentally altered or fundamentally affirmed in some way and ultimately shaped the healthcare system as we know it today.

Medicare's Inception and the Prospective Payment System

By the time the 1960s arrived, private insurance had been firmly established in the United States, with enrollees increasing over the course of the 1940s and 1950s from 20,662,000 in 1940 to 142,334,000 by 1960 (Thomasson, 2011, p. 1). There had been several attempts along the way to establish a national, government run insurance program in the decades preceding the 1960s, but were defeated due in large part to opposition from the American Medical Association (AMA), business and labor groups, as well as the private insurance industry, which was becoming more powerful during this time period. So, the healthcare landscape and power dynamic were firmly established and entrenched by the time President Kennedy and later President Johnson proposed and passed the legislation that created Medicare and Medicaid in 1965.

Watershed Year One: 1965

A driving factor in the passage of Medicare was, incidentally, costs. One of the ways in which private insurers like Blue Cross avoided averse selection in their enrollment pool was by linking their services to workplace insurance plans, which tended to cater to younger, healthier members of society. This indeed helped to keep their costs down as the elderly tended to need and use more medical resources. Unfortunately, once out of the workforce, and being potentially more ill, the elderly found it difficult to find or to afford private insurance during this period. This culminated with the passage of Medicare, which was in many respects the perfect opportunity for the federal government to enter the healthcare market. Historical opposition to both healthcare reform and government intervention acknowledged that medical care for the elderly and the poor would require government support. The lack of medical expertise among policy makers combined with the lack of any cost controls in addition to poor long-term cost projections ensured that Medicare would have numerous faults from the very beginning though. No one expected the rapid growth, in both the public and private sectors, brought about by the advent of Medicare.

When Medicare was rolled out in 1966 with around 19 million initial enrollees, the government had essentially adopted Blue Cross practice of reimbursing procedures at the cost identified by the provider on its annually submitted cost report. Physicians were paid on a fee-for-service basis and hospitals were reimbursed at whatever cost they incurred, with little oversight or uniformity among hospitals. Blue Cross was also used as an intermediary to receive billing and to make payments on behalf of Medicare. The lack of any cost controls or oversight left providers, essentially, in complete control of Medicare; the higher the costs that providers reported, the more that Medicare paid out. Almost from the very beginning of the program, policy makers knew this was going to be a problem. The Under Secretary of Health, Education, and Welfare at the time, Wilbur Cohen, remarked that, "The sponsors of Medicare, including myself, had to concede in 1965 that there would be no real controls over hospitals and physicians. I was required to promise before the final vote in the Executive Session of the House Ways and Means Committee that the Federal agency would exercise no control" (Mayes, 2006, p. 25). Leaving out any control mechanisms or regulatory oversight was an intentional attempt to accommodate physicians and hospitals and to convince them to support Medicare legislation. Consequently, costs far exceeded projections. The estimate for Medicare's first full year of operations was $1.3 billion but in reality ended up being nearly $4.6 billion. From that point forward, spending on the program doubled every 5 years. The efforts to alter the program and reign in the spending began almost immediately.

By 1973, healthcare costs had risen to 11% of the federal budget, up from 4% in 1965 (Hoffman, p. 5). Spending far outpaced normal growth and inflation. Between 1966 and 1976, the consumer price index increased 89%, while hospital costs grew at 345% (Mayes, 2006, p. 27). The problem during this period was that spending at the federal level was increasing too much at time when inflation was soaring, increasing from 3% in 1996 to nearly 6% in 1970 and up to almost 14% by 1980 (Bureau of Labor Statistics, 2014). Because of this, there existed a real need to reduce the budget, including runaway reimbursements to hospitals and other providers. The first attempt at modification came in 1972 in the form of Section 223 of the Social Security Amendments. This did two things: it expanded Medicare coverage for end-stage renal patients, the disabled, nursing homes, etc., while also differentiating hospital costs into routine and ancillary. This was done in order to determine what costs were unreasonable and to attempt to standardize payments for the routine costs, which up to this time were not uniformly paid out to providers. This legislation also made allowances for variable costs based on the severity of illness and differing degrees of technology usage in the form of the ancillary costs.

A number of other cost-containing measures were implemented at this time including wage and price freezes, certificate-of need requirements, hospital rate setting at the state level, Health Maintenance Organization (HMO) expansion and health planning, all implemented in an effort to control growth. While these measures had a modest effect in limiting the growth in hospital payments, they only treated the symptoms, not the root causes of the cost expansion. And in response, providers found ways to work around the new regulations, including hospitals modifying definitions and redefining what was routine and what was ancillary in efforts to maximize reimbursement. This period does mark the beginning period of an age of healthcare regulation, with the federal government beginning to exert more influence on the healthcare market.

Another important aspect of the 1972 Social Security Amendments was Section 222, which authorized the government to develop new reimbursement models. These new models were run by individual states and acted like testing grounds for the federal government to observe experiments and choose the most successful model to use nationwide. Turning states in to individual laboratories created the opportunity to try several different projects simultaneously and to innovate in ways not possible at the federal level. Perhaps the most successful of these state experiments, and the one that would form the foundation for the PPS, occurred in the state of New Jersey.

The conceptual groundwork for PPS was completed by professors at the University of Michigan and at Yale University. At the University of Michigan, William Dowling, PhD, published an article in 1974 that stated the cost of medical care was predictable and could be determined based on a number of predetermined factors. At the same time, at Yale University, John Thompson, RN, and Robert Fetter, PhD, developed diagnosis-related groups (DRGs) while studying variations in costs among hospitals in Connecticut. DRGs are a set of unique medical categories that can be used to measure a patient's consumption of resources. Initially, DRGs were designed to assess quality and improve patient care. Later, as they were adapted for state and local systems, they became a means of cost control without retaining the focus on quality of care and managing limited resources. New Jersey's program, Standard Hospital Accounting & Rate Evaluation (SHARE), sought to use DRGs to standardize hospital expenditures and reporting and required that all hospitals' budgets had to be within 10% of its peers' annual growth costs. SHARE began as a modest attempt to rationalize hospital payments, only regulating Medicare and Blue Cross initially. As hospitals in New Jersey began receiving less payments through Medicare and Blue Cross, they began shifting payments to insurers not regulated as a part of SHARE. As a result, 5 years into the program, insurers not under SHARE paid 30% more than Medicare and Blue Cross (Mayes, 2006, p. 36). This shifting of costs hinted that, again, this arrangement was not striking at the root of the costs increases, but instead was a measure hospitals and physicians could work around.

Impetus to implement PPS nationally came during the stagflation period of the late 1970s. From 1974 to 1977, hospital costs rose 15% annually, more than double the rate of inflation. President Carter introduced a bill that would have heavily regulated the healthcare sector, setting a cap on growth at 9%, effective on public and private payments alike. The Secretary of Health, Education & Welfare, Joseph Califano, said that hospitals had been abusing cost reimbursement leading to the exorbitant growth in costs and that it was time for the federal government to come in and regulate them. Opposition to this plan was strong and unified with many opposed to government regulation of the private healthcare sector. Additionally, hospitals announced a voluntary effort in which they would lower costs on their own, in place of regulation. This voluntary effort failed though, with costs growing at rates of 12.8% in 1978, 14.5% in 1979, 13% in 1980, and 18% in 1980, respectively (Mayes, 2006, pp. 39–40).

Hospitals' failure to voluntarily curb their costs severely impacted their credibility as a group and opened the door for federal regulators to come in with less opposition. The first of these measures, taken under President Reagan, was the Tax Equity and Fiscal Responsibility Act (TEFRA) in 1982. TEFRA had a number of cost-containment measures, including cuts in Medicare payments and limits on future growth rates. This piece of legislation effectively marked the end of retrospective reimbursement and served as a major shift in policy for cost containment. TEFRA also gave Congress leverage in bargaining during the next round of reform that would produce the PPS. Hospitals loathed the regulations contained within TEFRA and it moved them to a point where they could more easily accept PPS based on DRGs. In essence, TEFRA was a stepping stone to the passage and implementation of PPS in 1983.

One of the main architects of the DRG PPS was President Reagan's Secretary of Health & Human Services Richard Schweiker. Secretary Schweiker had extensive experience with New Jersey's experiment using DRGs and when tasked to reform Medicare used that experience in recommending DRGs. DRGs were also a natural evolution of the Section 223 cost limits that were introduced in 1972. A lot of the analytical work that went into determining those cost limits could be used as a basis for determining DRGs. In an effort to pass and implement this system before the most onerous provisions of TEFRA kicked in, the new PPS plan was developed at breakneck speed. This was needed for two reasons. First, there was finally the political will to pass such a reform and second, Social Security was in the middle of a major fiscal crisis.

As such, the rushed DRG PPS plan was added onto the Social Security bill and passed in early 1983. PPS was not debated and few in Congress actually understood it.

Watershed Year Two: 1983

Like with the original passage of Medicare, a confluence of several events led to the passing of payment reform in 1983. Increasing costs due to fee-for-service for physicians along with cost reimbursement for hospitals in addition to increases in technology created an untenable situation by the early 1980s. The passage of PPS was swift and fundamentally altered the power dynamic between the federal government and healthcare providers. And although DRGs had been used at the state level, it was uncertain what their implementation on a scale as large as Medicare would do and what the long-term consequences would be.

On the Road to Managed Care

The implementation of the PPS on Medicare in 1983 had far-reaching effects throughout healthcare. As the biggest individual payer in the market, the federal government now had the power to influence both the public and the private sector in unprecedented ways. PPS marked the biggest change in health policy since the passage of Medicare itself, fundamentally altering incentives. While PPS only applied to inpatient care, hospitals were able to ascertain which DRGs had the highest margins and where they could maximize profits by performing a particular procedure below the cost paid out by Medicare under the appropriate DRG. In the beginning years of PPS, hospitals were averaging near 15% margins on these procedures, which helped to make up for losses on Medicaid and charity care. Many hospitals actually found that they were better off under PPS than they were under cost reimbursement due in part to figuring out this system of high-margin/low-margin procedures.

Even with this high-/low-margin work-around, PPS appeared to be working. The rate of growth for total health expenditures, Medicare expenditures, and Medicare hospital payments all dropped significantly after the implementation of PPS. Before PPS, from 1980 to 1983, national expenditures averaged a 12.7% annual growth rate, whereas afterward, from 1984 to 1987, the rate dropped to 8.5%. Likewise, from 1980 to 1983, Medicare expenditures averaged a 15.0% annual growth rate compared to a 9.0% growth rate during the 1984 to 1987 period. Medicare hospital payments also showed a similar trend with a 16.2% average annual growth rate from 1990 to 1983 dropping to only 6.5% over 1984 to 1987 (Mayes, 2004, p. 154). So, on the surface, PPS seemed to be a resounding success. The new system had, for all intents and purposes, restrained Medicare's growth rate. However, the numbers masked other problems that were present and growing within the wider healthcare system.

First among these problems was that the basic incentive of providing more and not necessarily better care was left intact. Physicians were still paid on a fee-for-service basis, only now they and hospitals would choose the procedures with the best margins, such as cardiac surgery or neurosurgery, while devoting less time and resources on less profitable procedures, such as psychiatry and trauma care (Ryan, 2014, p. 729). Length of stay time for patients also decreased due to incentive paradigm favoring volume over quality. Additionally, hospitals also greatly expanded their outpatient services over this period, as PPS only applied to inpatient reimbursement. The number of hospitals that had outpatient services grew from 50% in 1983 at the inception of PPS to 87% by 1991. Hospital revenues from outpatient services doubled over this same time period, accounting for nearly a quarter of all hospital revenues by 1992 (National Council on Disability, 2013, p. 1).

The push for more outpatient care coincided with reimbursement rates being continually slashed and hospitals becoming more and more financially desperate. From Figure 2.3, the healthy margins that hospitals had enjoyed in the early years of PPS had begun to erode by the late 1980s. Congress consistently used PPS reimbursement cuts as a tool to balance deficits. This was seen as an easier alternative to cutting services for Medicare beneficiaries, which would have led to a host of political problems. Congress justified the cuts to hospitals based on the margins they reported, which created a contentious environment where hospitals tried to withhold data to avoid cuts. All in all, PPS reimbursement reductions were done without a focus on hospital or patient needs, only fiscal concerns were kept in mind. By 1992, margins to hospitals eroded to –2.6% (Prospective Payment Assessment Commission [ProPAC], 1994, p. 56), down from double-digit margins in the early years of the program. In 1984, only 16.8% of hospitals lost money on their Medicare

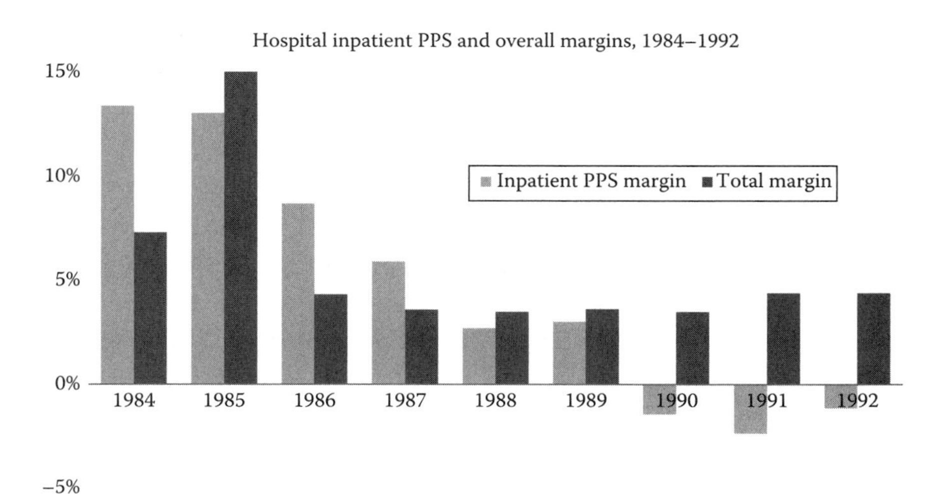

Figure 2.3 Hospital inpatient margins. (Modified from Prospective Payment Assessment Commission [ProPAC], Medicare and the American health care system, Report to the Congress, June 1994, pp. 40 and 56.)

population, but by 1992, this number had risen to 60.0% (Mayes, 2004, p. 156).

It is clear that while PPS curtailed the excessive growth rates that had plagued Medicare preceding its introduction, it did little to influence or change hospital spending. Hospitals' costs-per-case grew at an average of 8.6% annually (more than twice the inflation rate) between 1986 and 1992, even as inpatient PPS margins dwindled and pressures to cut costs increased (Mayes, 2004, p. 158). While many hospitals did begin putting into place efforts to curtail their own costs, many began simply shifting the losses they were incurring to private insurance. The magnitude of this cost shifting is debated, with some, like Chapin White, PhD, arguing in *Health Affairs* that instead of providers shifting costs when Medicare lowers reimbursement rates, they instead implement cost-containing measures. He also argues that private insurers follow Medicare's lead and constrict their own payments more than they would have done otherwise (White, 2013, pp. 935–936). Exclusively cost shifting or exclusively cost containing was probably not the response of most hospitals, instead a combination of the two was the most likely response. One thing is agreed upon though, the disparities between private and public plans ballooned during this period.

Cost shifting was not a new phenomenon to subsidize unreimbursed costs. Earlier in this chapter, we saw that this happened in New Jersey when they implemented their SHARE program. The difference now was that the amount shifted to private insurers was no longer palatable. From 1984 to 1993, the average annual increase in the per capita cost of private insurance was 22.7% more than Medicare. Hospitals payment-to-cost ratio for Medicare in 1992 was only 0.89, where for every dollar they spent on a Medicare procedure, they would only be reimbursed 89 cents. Conversely, private insurers' ratio was 1.31 (Mayes, 2004, pp. 158–159). Businesses began to feel this shifting on their bottom lines. Employee premiums doubled from 1984 to 1991, from $1645 to $3605 (National Council on Disability, 2013, p. 1). The rising cost of private insurance led many companies to reduce benefits, require employees to pay a larger share of their premiums, offer to pay health costs instead of offering insurance, or, as was gaining popularity, move their employees into managed care plans. From Figure 2.4, traditional indemnity insurance provided to workers plummeted from 73% in 1988 to only 10% by 1999. Costs were reasonably controlled due to the transition to managed care though. From 1993 to 1998, healthcare costs increased by 31%, the slowest rate in 40 years (Emanuel, 2012, p. 2263).

Managed care in this form ultimately failed, and costs resumed their exponential growth patterns. From 1999 to 2010, costs increased by 102% (Emanuel, 2012, p. 2264). The backlash against managed care during the 1990s is well documented. Physicians and patients alike felt alienated and the opaque nature of managed care left them without satisfactory explanations. Under these managed care plans, physicians were often

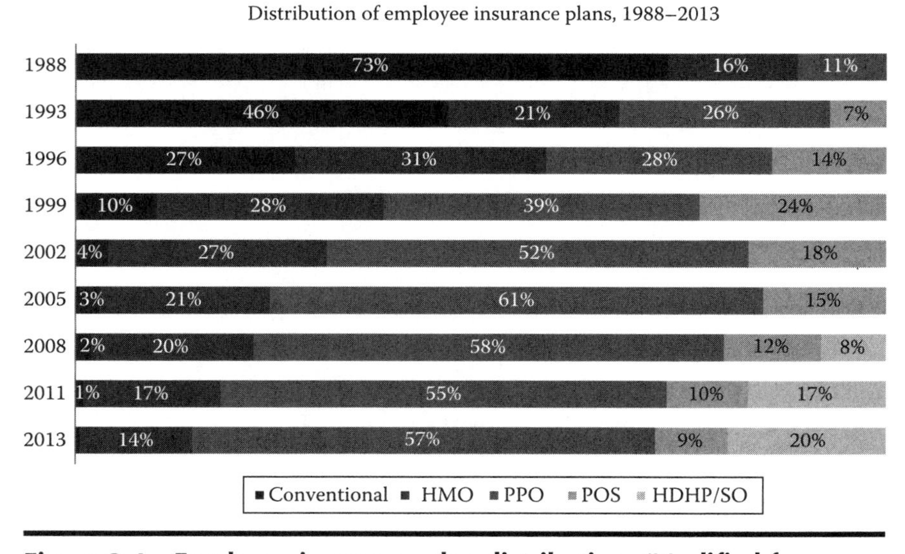

Figure 2.4 Employee insurance plan distribution. (Modified from Claxton, G. et al., *Employer Health Benefits: 2013 Annual Survey*, Kaiser Family Foundation, Health Research & Educational Trust, and NORC at the University of Chicago, p. 65.)

left out of narrow networks, had to negotiate down payments to secure contracts, and were required to obtain authorization before performing many procedures. This was combined with patients' dislike of being denied certain tests and procedures in addition to having to change networks and doctors whenever changing jobs or switching insurance. Managed care truly failed though because, like previous cost-containment strategies for both public and private insurance, it only focused on paying less. There was little managed care in the sense of integrating care and working with physicians to deliver more efficient, value-based care. In fact, by severely restricting networks of providers, this was more difficult to do in some respects. Additionally, by the late 1990s, the economy was booming, unemployment was low, and businesses felt it necessary to relax their managed care plans to satisfy their employees, even at the expense of costs increasing again as they had before.

Watershed Year Three: 1997

Three pieces of legislation passed during late 1990s and early 2000s, the Balanced Budget Act (BBA) of 1997, the Balanced Budget Refinement Act (BBRA) of 1999, and the Benefits Improvement and Protection Act (BIPA) of 2000, all had profound impacts upon the system, sometimes in slightly contradictory ways. The BBA introduced new PPSs for Medicare, namely those for outpatient and post-acute services. Both of these fields had grown tremendously in the wake of the implementation of the inpatient PPS and were seen as areas where reform was needed to maintain the solvency of the program. While the BBA helped to contribute to historically low growth in spending, some felt that the cuts made were too severe and were put into place too quickly. As a result, BBRA and BIPA were passed to temper and moderate some of the changes made by the BBA. This included some kickbacks to providers and may have contributed to the resumption of the high annual growth patterns that returned in the early 2000s (White, 2008, pp. 796–797).

The BBA was instrumental though, in that it reconfirmed the American healthcare policy and the means of delivery and reimbursement of healthcare services utilizing multi-venues of care. The BBA, in effect, established the "hub and spoke model" (Figure 2.5) wherein length of stay and payments were restricted within the most expensive venue, that is the short-term acute hospital, with ratified reimbursement structures for post-acute inpatient and outpatient venues of care. As outpatient and post-acute settings expanded exponentially after the introduction of inpatient PPS, care delivery sites shifted from acute inpatient (hub) to the spoke model. As care shifted from the hub to the spokes, this minimized the most expensive form of care (i.e. acute hospital inpatient) and was, in and of itself, a form of cost containment. In essence, this shifting was a recalibration of intent and need of service delivery venue, moving care into more appropriate settings. Murer has supported and helped to define this model (Table 2.1) over the course of the past 30 years.

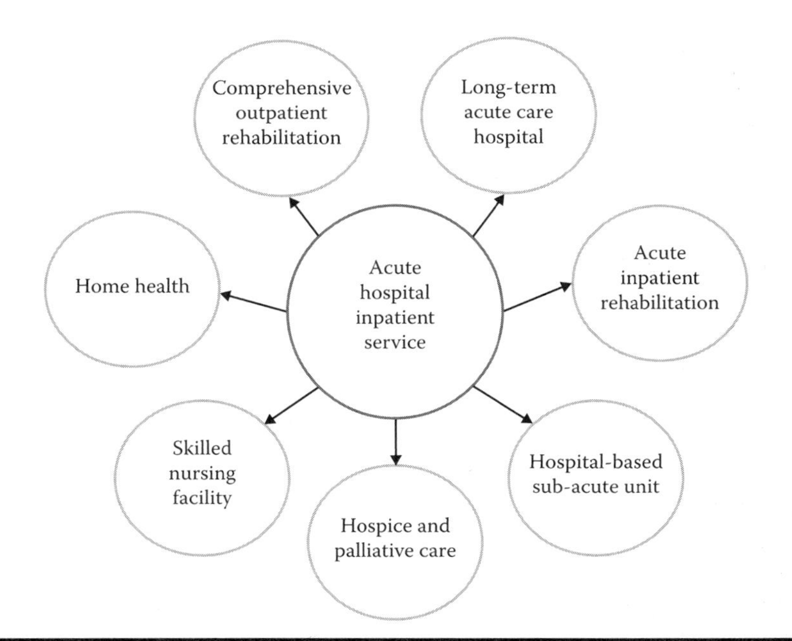

Figure 2.5 Hub and spoke model.

Table 2.1 Venues of Care

	ICU	*Acute*	*Long-Term Acute Care Hospital*	*Rehabilitation Unit*	*Skilled/ Subacute*	*Outpatient/ CORF*
Type of facility	Unit of short-term hospital	Short-term acute care hospital	Long-term acute care freestanding or hospital within a hospital	Unit or hospital	Unit or facility	Outpatient services
Payment structure	Prospective payment system under DRGs	Prospective payment system under DRGs	PPS exempt under LTC-DRGs	PPS exempt under case mix groups	PPS exempt under MDS/RUG categories	CPT codes
Direct nursing hours per patient day	Average 14–19 hours	Average 7.25–8 DNH	Average 8–11 DNH	Average 5.5 DNH	Average 4–4.5 DNH	Average 1.5 hours
Physician	Daily or more with specialist contact	7 days per week	7 days per week	Minimum standard 3 days/week but generally seen 5+ days/week	Intermittent. average 3 days per week	Intermittent. Less than 1 day per week

(*Continued*)

Table 2.1 (*Continued*) Venues of Care

	ICU	*Acute*	*Long-Term Acute Care Hospital*	*Rehabilitation Unit*	*Skilled/ Subacute*	*Outpatient/ CORF*
Condition	May change by the minute	May change by the day	May change by the week or day	May change by the week	May change by the week	Medically stable
Stability	Patient in crisis	Possibility for crisis	Possibility for crisis	Medically stable	Newly stable	Medically stable
ALOS	1–5 days	3–5 days	18–35 days	10–22 days	7–20 days	2–6 weeks
Average medicate payment	$1900 per diem	$1500 per diem	$1300–$1700 per diem	$750 per diem	$350 Per diem	$3000 per discharge

The year 1997 was indeed a watershed year given that Congress had the opportunity to fundamentally change the American healthcare delivery model. Congress could have defined or redefined the delivery mechanism in a number of ways such as dominant and/or singular use of the short-term acute care hospital, but chose to reinforce and reaffirm the acute—post-acute paradigm. It should be noted that determination of a nation's healthcare delivery policy is particular to the social mores and politics of that country. Indeed, there is no perfect model.

As previously discussed, the 1997 BBA ensured decentralization of service delivery through the hub and spoke model, which concentrated the most expensive diagnostic, episodic, and critical care within the inpatient hospital setting. Since valuable resources can be lost on rote motion in a more centralized system, where beds remain occupied beyond medical necessity for an acute level of care and diagnostic tests are ordered simply because the bed is filled, the mandate for effective and timely movement of patients along the continuum of care results in cost efficiencies and cost containment.

Whenever a system is subject to extensive review and is subsequently modified, in many respects, the system is revalidated with each subsequent action. In healthcare, every October, on the federal fiscal year, Medicare modifies reimbursement per DRG, and in doing this, the general model is reinforced. The BBA was instrumental in that it formalized the healthcare model that had been evolving since the passage of Medicare in 1965 under President Johnson's Great Society.

Going Forward: Opportunities and Barriers

Watershed Year Four: 2010

Being in the midst of a current reform environment, brought about as part of the Affordable Care Act (ACA), the situation is complex and ever changing today. There are some interesting parallels with the aforementioned history that signal that the time is ripe for broader payment reform. As with TEFRA in 1982, the ACA has also set permanent limits of Medicare growth and has cut payment rates to nearly all providers, excluding physicians. TEFRA was used as leverage in passing payment reform that was seen as less burdensome and from that, PPS was born. Likewise, the ACA contains many provisions that hint that a move away from prospective payment and away from fee-for-service is coming sometime in the future. The ACA includes value-based payment programs for hospitals, post-acute care facilities, and physicians alike. Because of this, many expect the ACA to facilitate the adoption of pay-for-performance measures in an effort to get away from fee-for-service (Cromwell, 2011, pp. 14–25). Performance can be defined as quality, reporting, efficiency, and/or value and as we have seen with CCMAs, while there are still regulatory roadblocks in place, they offer a chance to change incentives by tying compensation to performance.

The future for developing these new models looks bright indeed. Both public and private insurers have experimented with new models in response to healthcare reform (and in some cases even beforehand). Blue Cross Blue Shield developed the Alternative Quality Contract that combines a per-patient budget with an incentive structure. The potential cost savings that Blue Cross Blue Shield has projected are quite impressive (Alliance for Health Reform, 2012, p. 10). In the public sector, as we saw in Chapter 1, the CMS Innovation Center has also been experimenting with accountable care, bundled payments, and on and on. Medicare has also expanded its use of managed care recently with encouraging results. From 2003 to 2009, enrollment in Medicare Advantage increased from 4.6 to 12.8 million. The latter number represented over 25% of Medicare beneficiaries in 2009. Studies on Medicare Advantage also suggest that beneficiaries enrolled in managed care use fewer and more appropriate services than those enrolled in traditional Medicare (Landon, 2012, pp. 2613–2614). And while it does appear that the excessive growth (healthcare cost growth above that of normal GDP growth) which plagued Medicare for so long appears to have been brought under control (Figure 2.6), it is critical the next steps in delivery and payment are studied and put forth. Much in the way that DRGs were first studied on a state scale, expanded for use nationwide, and ultimately led to wider use of managed care, innovations put forth by CMS in the future will have the similar ability to transform healthcare, public and private alike.

In order for new delivery and payment systems to work though, the renewed push toward managed care provided by the ACA must be combined with the lessons learned from PPS

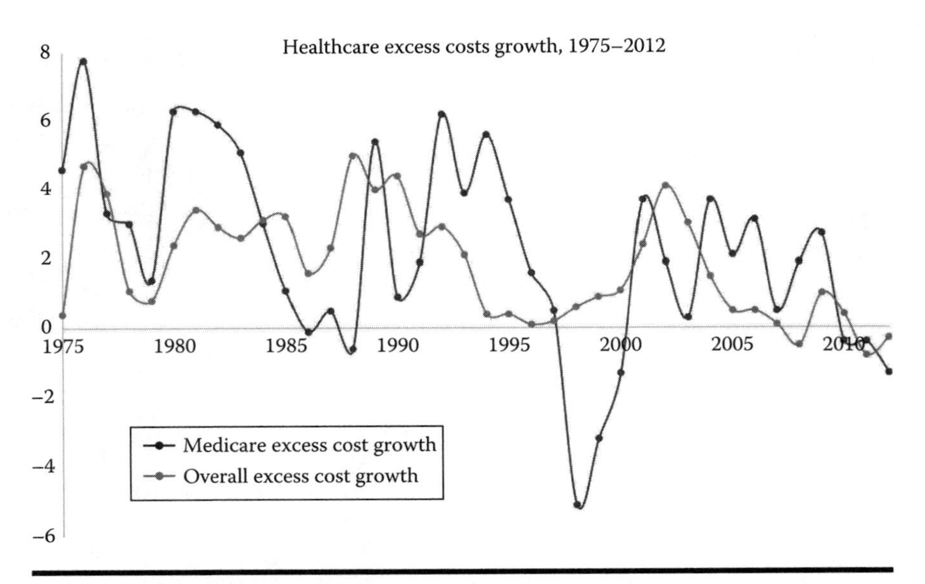

Figure 2.6 Historical healthcare costs growth. (Modified from Centers for Medicare & Medicaid Services, National Health Expenditure Accounts, National health expenditures by type of service and source of funds, CY 1960–2012, Woodlawn, MD, January 7, 2014—NHE tables; Congressional Budget Office, The 2014 long-term budget outlook, July 2014 Release, July 25, 2014, https://www.cbo.gov/about/privacy.)

and the managed care backlash of the 1990s. Cost containment cannot be the sole focus of reform; it must be done in a holistic manner, one that fundamentally alters and aligns incentives and focuses on quality and value instead of the bottom line alone. Cost-saving measures need to be combined with the better data, guidelines, and metrics that we have today and use them to improve physician management, control, and coordination, instead of restricting them as was done in the 1990s. Only when this coupling is complete and only when payment and delivery models are designed with root issues in mind, beyond just cost, can we develop a truly integrated and effective healthcare system. This is what the ACA has hinted at doing and is the function for which we have designed CCMAs to perform. We are at a time when opportunity and necessity have converged, creating a unique environment to work and to innovate in.

Of course, there are barriers. As we have seen throughout this chapter, the healthcare system has a lot of historical baggage. Having such a fragmented and decentralized system means that it cannot be changed easily, even if it is in the best interest of those involved to do so. And each round of reforms adds yet another layer onto the system, adding to the bureaucracy and to the scale. Since everyone in the country relies on the continued functioning of the healthcare system for the continued functioning of their individual health, the only reform measures that can be done are the ones that add to or alter it in some measured way. So, it is very difficult to reverse incentives system-wide when the system must remain largely intact during the reform process. And it is difficult to challenge the silo mind-set and entrenched interests involved in this market when political and fiscal concerns superseded clinical ones. But the historical moments of opportunity and the watershed years do come. It is imperative we continue innovating and developing new models on the local, regional, and statewide levels so that when one of these moments does arrive, we are prepared.

References

Alliance for Health Reform. *High and Rising Costs of Health Care in the U.S. 2012*, Washington, DC, 2012. http://www.allhealth.org.

Boccuti, C. and Moon, M. Comparing Medicare and private insurers: Growth rates in spending over three decades. *Health Affairs* 22(2) (2003):230–237.

Bureau of Labor Statistics. *Consumer Price Index*. United States Department of Labor, Washington, DC, August 19, 2014.

Centers for Medicare & Medicaid Services. National Health Expenditure Accounts. National health expenditures by type of service and source of funds, CY 1960–2012, Woodlawn, MD, January 7, 2014.

Claxton, G., Rae, M., Panchal, N., Damico, A., Bostick, N., Kenward, K., and Whitmore, H. *Employer Health Benefits: 2013 Annual Survey*. Kaiser Family Foundation, Health Research & Educational Trust, and NORC at the University of Chicago, 2013.

Congressional Budget Office. The 2014 long-term budget outlook. July 2014 Release, July 25, 2014. https://www.cbo.gov/about/privacy. (Accessed August 25, 2014.)

Cromwell, J., Trisolini, M. G., Pope, G. C., Mitchell, J. B., and Greenwald, L. M. *Pay for Performance in Health Care: Methods and Approaches*. Research Triangle Institute, Research Triangle Park, NC, 2011.

Draper, D. A., Hurley, R. E., Lesser, C. S., and Strunk, B. C. The changing face of managed care. *Health Affairs* 21(1) (2002):11–23.

Emanuel, E. J. Why accountable care organizations are not 1990s managed care redux. *The Journal of the American Medical Association* 307(21) (2012):2263–2264.

Hoffman, C. National Health Insurance—A brief history of reform efforts in the U.S. Kaiser Family Foundation's Commission on Medicaid and the Uninsured, March 2009. http://www.kff.org.

Landon, B. E., Zaslavsky, A. M., Saunders, R. C., Pawlson, L. G., Newhouse, J. P., and Ayanian, J. Z. Analysis of Medicare advantage HMOs compared with traditional Medicare shows lower use of many services during 2003–09. *Health Affairs* 31(12) (2012):2609–2617.

Mayes, R. Causal chains and cost shifting: How Medicare's rescue inadvertently triggered the managed-care revolution. *The Journal of Policy History* 16(2) (2004):144–174.

Mayes, R. The origins, development, and passage of Medicare's revolutionary prospective payment system. *Journal of the History of Medicine and Allied Sciences* 62(1) (2006):21–55.
National Council on Disability. Appendix B. A brief history of managed care, 2013. http://www.ncd.gov/publications/2013/20130315/20130513_AppendixB. (Accessed August 25, 2014.)
Prospective Payment Assessment Commission (ProPAC). Medicare and the American health care system. Report to the Congress, June 1994.
Reschovsky, J. D., Hadley, J., and Landon, B. E. Effects of compensation methods and physician group structure on physicians' perceived incentives to alter services to patients. *Health Services Research* 41(4) (2006):1200–1220.
Ryan, A. M. and Mushlin, A. L. The affordable care act's payment reforms and the future of hospitals. *Annals of Internal Medicine* 160 (2014):729–730.
Scanlon, W. J. The future of Medicare hospital payment. *Health Affairs* 25(1) (2006):70–80.
Thomasson, M. Health insurance in the United States. EH.Net Encyclopedia. Economic History Association, Tucson, AZ, September 3, 2011.
White, C. Why did Medicare spending growth slow down? *Health Affairs* 27(3) (2008):793–802.
White, C. Contrary to cost-shift theory, lower Medicare hospital payment rates for inpatient care lead to lower private payment rates. *Health Affairs* 32(5) (2013):935–943.
White, C. and Ginsburg, P. B. Slower growth in Medicare spending–Is this the new normal? *The New England Journal of Medicine* 366 (2012):1073–1075.

Chapter 3

Clinical Co-Management as the Bridge Toward Bundled Care

Push from Fee-for-Service toward Bundling

From the first two chapters, we have seen how the inefficiencies present in the healthcare system have developed over time and why there is a real and urgent need for Clinical Co-Management Agreements (CCMAs). What does the future hold for the American healthcare delivery system? And how can we get there given the tools at our disposal? The long-term answer to that question is BUNDLING. By completely integrating care over a continuum of providers, bundling payment offers exciting possibilities to improve care, rein in costs, and realize better efficiencies in the healthcare system. Moving from the historical and ingrained fee-for-service (FFS) environment to one of bundling is perhaps one of the greatest healthcare challenges facing us in the next decade. CCMA offers a reasonable and achievable solution. CCMA serves as the precursor to fully bundled care and can serve as the bridge from FFS to bundling. CCMAs are the beginning point and the catalyst for providers to lay the groundwork for making bundling feasible and financially attractive. By emphasizing the collection and usage of data, along with the improved coordination of historically separated and siloed providers, CCMAs can begin to bridge what seems like the irreconcilable gulf between FFS and bundling (Figure 3.1).

The financial incentives to move from an FFS system to a bundled one already exist, albeit theoretically. FFS has been a primary contributor to the exponential growth rate in healthcare costs that the United States has experienced over the past 60 years. From Chapter 2, FFS encourages volume growth, where providers get paid more to do more, and this has led directly to the overuse of potentially unnecessary treatment. This system has also fostered a fragmented environment in which providers are paid separately to do independent work. Under such a system, there is little impetus to coordinate or integrate care among providers, which leads to waste, inefficiencies, and reduced quality of care for patients. In contrast to that, bundling provides for a single payment per episode of care in which providers then split among themselves. The more efficient the care, the lower the total costs incurred by the providers, and the higher the margins earned from the bundled payment. This will lead to efficiency gains in which providers are incentivized to work in conjunction with one another in order to maximize their individual returns. Some projections have put the reduction in healthcare spending, including both inpatient and outpatient services, at over 5%

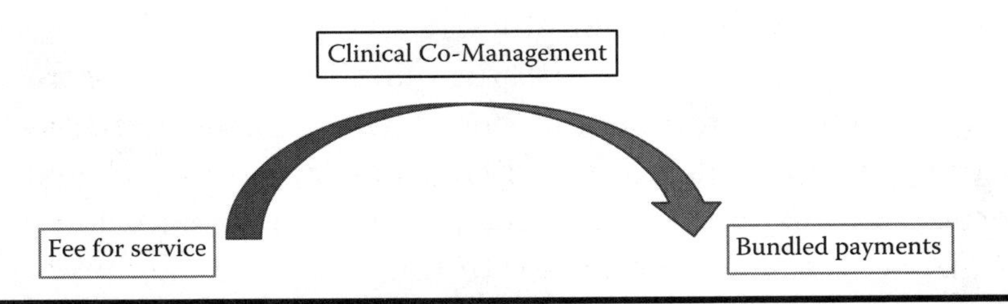

Figure 3.1 Clinical Co-Management as a bridge.

for the period of 2010–2019 if a bundling scheme were to be implemented (Hussey, 2009, p. 2110).

This is one of the reasons why bundling is being promoted in the current reform environment. The Affordable Care Act contains several initiatives regarding bundling, including a Medicare bundling pilot program called the Bundled Payments for Care Improvement Initiative (BPCI). Under BPCI, the CMS Innovation Center created four bundling models: Retrospective Acute Care Hospital Stay Only, Retrospective Acute Care Hospital Stay plus Post-Acute Care, Retrospective Post-Acute Care Only, and Acute Care Hospital Stay Only. Nearly 50 episodes of care have been identified under this plan and over 500 providers have signed up for the 3-year pilot, which began in 2013. Individual states along with private insurers are also experimenting with bundling. Arkansas has introduced the Arkansas Health Care Payment Improvement Initiative (APII), which is a combined government and private sector initiative to introduce episodic bundling within the state. Tennessee has also introduced a similar initiative with the Tennessee Health Care Innovation Initiative, which includes three strategies: primary care transformation, episodes of care, and long-term services and support. In the private sector, the PROMETHEUS (Provider Payment Reform for Outcomes, Margins, Evidence, Transparency Hassle-reduction, Excellence, Understandability and Sustainability) bundled payment plan was created with support from the Robert Wood Johnson Foundation and is currently being tested in a pilot study. Insurers like Blue Cross Blue Shield have also been experimenting with bundled payments in some states for limited services like pregnancies and deliveries, joint replacements, and breast cancer.

In the 1990s, there was a similar push away from traditional FFS in hopes of controlling costs. That was the failed move to capitation. Where full capitation came up short, in both the practical and public relations (PR) sense, bundling appears poised to have learned from those mistakes. Under full capitation, providers were, in essence, penalized for caring for sicker patients due to the flat payment for all care, regardless of severity. Thus, more resources were required for patients with more severe illnesses or a higher number of comorbidities, and this led to a kind of adverse selection by providers seeking to avoid caring for these more costly patients. Bundling, on the other hand, ensures that providers do not have the same motivation to avoid taking on sicker patients as they had under capitation. A bundled payment will only pay for one, specific episode of care meaning that providers will not have to expend additional uncompensated resources as under capitation. So while the main pitfalls of capitation are avoided under bundling, the benefits are still realized. Bundling also allows risk to be shared in ways not possible under capitation as it distinguishes between performance risk and insurance risk.

Whereas capitation puts complete financial risk on providers, bundling allows performance risk to be separated from insurance risk. This is important for several reasons. First, insurance risk can be shifted from providers to payers. This is simply the risk that a patient will become sick, require medical services, and is essentially what health insurance is designed to cover. The other portion of risk though, the performance risk, stays with providers. This risk covers what providers have control over and creates a platform not only to share risk but to share accountability as well. From this spring the possibilities of paying for performance. Bundling is an attractive delivery system because of the opportunity of tying provider performance and quality of care provided to compensation received. In a bundled payment agreement, providers will earn more for higher-quality work, thereby incentivizing them to coordinate their activities with one another and provide the best care possible at the lowest prices possible. Performance risk (e.g. case efficiency, infection rates) and insurance risk (e.g. chronic or unanticipated illness) can be combined in a pay-for-performance setting to help improve process reliability, clinical quality, and illness prevention. Pay for performance and quality-based incentives are also seen as a way to improve financial accountability, which is critical moving forward in controlling costs.

In addition to the benefit of tying performance to quality of care, bundling also has the potential for reining in costs while promoting equal or higher quality of care. Bundling is still a relatively new and evolving payment system, with many pilot projects still in the trial phase, but the results that do exist are promising in terms of cost and quality. Blue Cross Blue Shield in North Carolina, in conjunction with CaroMont Health, instituted a bundle payment based upon the PROMETHEUS system for knee replacements. From a 1-year study, the bundled plan led to a savings of 8%–10% per case (Delbanco, 2014, p. 1). Likewise, Geisinger Health System in Pennsylvania tested a ProvenCare bundled payment model for coronary artery bypass graft surgery (CABG). Results from the ProvenCare model showed a 10% reduction in readmissions in addition to a decreased length of stay for patients (Delbanco, 2014, p. 1). Medicare also tested a bundled CABG payment system in the 1990s, with similar levels of success. From 1991 to 1996, Medicare saved approximately 10% on CABG procedures in the program, translating to over $40 million in savings while maintaining the same levels of quality (Center for Medicare & Medicaid Services, 1998, pp. 1–2). While these are narrow studies, they show that bundling can work providing for cost savings and reduction in admissions while not negatively impacting the levels of quality. These are exactly the aims of healthcare reform attempts and what the system as a whole needs moving into the future.

Difficulties of Bundled Care: Lessons from Previous Bundling Attempts

With so many positive benefits, why then has the adoption of bundling not been more widespread? The answer to this is two pronged, with part of the problem rooted in the conceptual framework of the healthcare system and the other being the technical construction of the bundling schemes themselves. For the conceptual part of this, healthcare remains embroiled within capitalism. This creates an environment with an ongoing tension between the need for providers to cut costs on one hand and perform more procedures to remain profitable on the other hand. Physicians and hospitals alike are dependent upon the need to do more and on the financial realities of healthcare under FFS; these may not align the best utilization of resources or the best care for an individual patient. FFS has contributed to this silo mind-set and has never disposed providers or payers to think in an integrated manner. That is why today, for a given patient, an internist, gastroenterologist, radiologist, anesthesiologist, surgeon, and pathologist may work collaboratively and in unison to treat a specific condition, but each physician's work is still viewed as and paid for separately. As such, we have a system today where each provider and each specialty are entities unto themselves instead of fully integrated parts of a greater medical whole. Convincing each of these separate entities to move away from FFS, receive a bundled payment as part of a coordinated team, and split the work and payment equably presents a great challenge going forward with bundling.

Establishing bundles also comes with a number of technical difficulties that must be agreed upon in advance by all parties. Primary among them are defining and managing costs. Without reliable or predictable costs for the procedures or treatments involved, it is impossible to construct a bundled payment. There needs to be verifiable cost of an episode of care based upon uniform methodology for cost accounting and consistent application. That methodology, once established, needs to manage variances based on a number of circumstances in order to ensure that an episode cost does not exceed bundled reimbursement. Once cost has been dealt with, all services included in a bundle need to be defined and all language and definitions within needs to be agreed upon.

It may be easier to begin bundling procedures that already have reliable metrics and predictable outcomes than procedures or treatments where provider roles may not be so clearly defined or outcomes as predictable. Accountability for patient care and reimbursement must also be agreed upon prior to care. And last, the continued collection of data, each provider performing his or her respective task, and performance payments are all critical technical components for the continued functioning of the bundled payment.

Another difficulty in constructing a bundled payment is the verification and validation of collected data. Evidence-based medicine should undoubtedly be at the core of constructing bundles, but here lies some difficulties. When medical decisions are "sales based" instead of "evidence based" patient care suffers. Decisions that are not made based upon best practices or accepted medical knowledge usually falter without buy-in from the physicians actually performing the procedures. Beyond the administrator/physician divide, the evidence for some procedures effectiveness may be unclear. As mentioned in the previous paragraph, some procedures or treatments better lend themselves to the collection of data or for the reliability of outcomes. And some providers may or may not have reliable and standardized protocols already in place. If not, the effectiveness or the best way to collect data may not be understood well enough to successfully construct a bundled payment mechanism. Until those measurement techniques and outcomes are improved and standardized, it will remain difficult to put evidence at the center of a bundle. The fact that as an integral component of bundles, this also means evidence is the basis of reimbursement payments and performance compensation. Improving the collection of data, the subsequent usage of that data, and the reliability of a given procedure needs to be given top priority before bundling can feasibly be implemented.

An example that illustrates the difficulties of the current healthcare system is medical tourism. The concept of medical tourism is not new. Individuals who are uninsured, underinsured, or who want elective procedures not covered by insurance plans may choose to travel to another country for medical care. As the costs of procedures have expeditiously grown in the United States, so has medical tourism abroad. Individuals have found similar levels of quality for reduced prices and some have been able to bundle procedures or prices to make the prospect of going abroad more attractive. This translates directly to revenue and market share losses for providers. Medical tourism is expected to grow from 750,000 patients per year in 2007 to 15.7 million by 2017. The loss of revenue will likewise grow from $15.9 billion in 2007 to somewhere between $228.5 and $599.5 billion by 2017 if the growth trend holds true (Fottler et al., 2004, p. 51).

Interestingly enough, another type of medical tourism has grown in recent years, starkly illustrating the need for payment reform, transparency, and bundling options in the United States. This is the domestic medical tourism industry in which large, self-insured corporations contract with specific providers to offer one of more procedures to all employees around the country. The companies negotiate a bundled price for a procedure and usually save between 20% and 50% over a traditional FFS contracted price. Then, all employees in need of the particular procedure are flown to the contracted provider's facility for treatment. Companies such as Wal-Mart, Boeing, PepsiCo, and Lowe's have implemented such bundled arrangements for some procedures such as hip and joint replacements. Over 40% of patients have indicated that they would travel for care if they could achieve 50% cost savings (Fottler et al., 2014, p. 52). The rise in these bundled agreements shows that the healthcare system is out of kilter. High-quality care for lower prices is possible, but it takes a massive amount of bargaining power and leverage to implement.

While large corporations appear to be having some success with bundles, many of the pilot studies mentioned earlier in the chapter have encountered major hurdles to successful implementation. These difficulties illuminate the areas that need to be addressed for bundles to be effective and widely adopted by providers and payers alike. The first of these examples involves PROMETHEUS. As was discussed earlier in the chapter, PROMETHEUS is a private sector pilot program created with support from the Robert Wood Johnson Foundation, which had been described as the most exciting and innovative attempt to bring bundling into mainstream practice. Unfortunately, PROMETHEUS has not lived up to that billing, but its difficulties provide valuable insight into areas of concern that must be addressed. The PROMETHEUS plan initially defined 13 bundles ranging from chronic conditions like diabetes to acute conditions like acute myocardial infarction to procedures like hip replacement. It was then initially instituted at three pilot sites in Pennsylvania, Illinois, and Michigan. By 2011 though, 3 years after the start of the pilot, none of the three sites had been successful in executing a bundled payment contract between payers and providers, or in actually using PROMETHEUS as a viable payment method.

Key issues included defining the bundles, defining the payment method, implementing quality measurement, determining accountability, engaging providers, and care redesign. Individuals working to implement PROMETHEUS found that it was difficult to define and apply case rate definitions to data. Both sides were hesitant to execute contracts; payers would not pay out shared savings and providers would not change the delivery of care before the change in payments was made. Providers also found it difficult to define the accountability of differing roles and from that determine proper payments. Although support for the program was high with administrators, it was difficult to obtain physician interest and as such, buy-in was rather low overall.

All of the aforementioned hurdles sprout from the fact that PROMETHEUS, like all bundling, is built upon the existing FFS system and adds another layer of complexity to that system. All bundles under PROMETHEUS were identified using existing claims information that providers report for insurance. Pilot sites found that bundling was very sensitive to the quality of information they had and that none of it, like insurance claims, had been designed with bundling in mind. PROMETHEUS also used different language and lingo that slowed the adoption process. It was successful in several important aspects though, including raising awareness for the need for better measurement and data collection, opening lines of communication among stakeholders, and engaging them in conversations about improving care. In general, it changed some providers' perspective on how to improve care through improved coordination (Hussey, 2011, p. 2120).

Another example comes from the Integrated Healthcare Association (IHA) of California, a nonprofit association that consists of health plans, hospitals, ambulatory surgery centers, physician organizations, and vendors. Beginning in 2011 and using a consensus-oriented approach, IHA created a steering committee with members from the involved providers. From there, the committee determined episodes for knee and hip replacement surgery. Like with the PROMETHEUS plan, an array of issues prevented these bundles from wide adoption and implementation. Only three of the six original health plans along with two of the original eight hospitals executed contracts for bundled care. The problems cited were that, "…the complexity of multiparty contracting, bundle definition, risk sharing, gain sharing, care redesign, information technology, and payment proved insurmountable. Allocation of risk for the cost of adverse events was often particularly contentious, becoming at times 'a largely unexpressed contest of wills between the health plans and hospitals,' according to an Integrated Healthcare Association report" (Cunningham, 2014, p. 736). IHA, like PROMETHEUS, illustrates some of the intractable problems of trying to set up bundles in an FFS environment and points to the need to an intermediate delivery system to facilitate the transition.

Clinical Co-Management as the Precursor to Bundling

Healthcare delivery, like a language, is a continuum containing numerous dialects and nuances. At first glance, moving from an FFS system to a bundled system is in many ways like learning a new language. The grammar and the syntax may be different. New sounds and new words may be unfamiliar and unintelligible at first. Fortunately, there is an important nuance in this continuum between language and dialect, between unintelligibility and understanding. That nuance is the CCMA, which serves as a kind of standard language, connecting FFS to bundling. For example, Arabic spoken in Morocco may be unintelligible in Lebanon, yet they are connected by Standard Arabic making different ends of a dialect spectrum part of the greater whole instead of separate languages. Likewise, CCMAs speak to both FFS and bundling bringing them both into a dialect spectrum, where they too would be considered separate languages otherwise. CCMAs as a kind of mutually intelligible dialect means that it will be easier to learn and adapt to new dialects as healthcare moves away from FFS, making the transition more smooth than it would have otherwise been going straight to bundling.

The first way in which CCMAs change the FFS language is through data. Without the validation of data, there can be no bundling. CCMAs serve as the tool to begin collecting, organizing, and understanding data. Both parties agree on what data need to be tracked, what data are and are not currently being measured, and how to accurately capture those data going forward. Then, metrics are agreed upon and established, baselines are measured and compared against national benchmarks, measurement techniques are refined and codified, and with this entire process, data are validated and built upon to include more and more measures. Once this validation occurs and data are accurately captured, quality-based payment can be introduced and performance can be compared both historically over time as well against like providers. This moves the partnership into the realm of trust, which is a necessary component between hospitals and physicians for bundling to work. This is a verifiable trust, backed up by data. It moves beyond a one-on-one, personal type of trust and in doing so ties people together contractually, financially, and professionally. In tying providers together in this manner, patient care naturally becomes more connected and integrated as well.

The need for trust speaks to the larger shift that is needed for bundling to be successful. Physician and hospital philosophy, culture, and morals all need to be in parallel in order to agree to and work under a payment scheme that is radically different from the status quo. Without CCMAs, bundling is really a chicken and the egg scenario; providers are unable to do a lot of the uncompensated work necessary to lay the foundation for bundling, but without it, there is no impetus to move away from FFS. CCMAs offer a middle ground and a realistic way to shift the language while being sensitive to the workings and the inertia of the current system. Focusing on the collecting and validation of data, the reliability of protocols and procedures, as well as performance and quality-based compensation, CCMAs begin the process of building trust and aligning disparate providers' interests and goals. As the intermediate step between FFS and full bundling, CCMA remains an effective vehicle to bridge this historical philosophical and financial divide.

References

Center for Medicare & Medicaid Services. Medicare heart bypass summary, 1998. http://www.cms.gov/Medicare/Demonstration-Projects/DemoProjectsEvalRpts/Medicare-Demonstrations-Items/CMS063472.html. (Accessed March 10, 2015.)

Cunningham, R. The payment reform paradox. *Health Affairs* 33(5) (2014):735–738.

Delbanco, S. The payment reform landscape: Bundled payment. *Health Affairs Blog*, July 2, 2014. http://healthaffairs.org/blog/2014/07/02/the-payment-reform-landscape-bundled-payment/. (Accessed March 10, 2015.)

Dredge, C. CMS movement to bundled payments. (August 2012):1–24. The Arkansas health care payment improvement initiative.

Fottler, M. D. et al. Can inbound and domestic medical tourism improve your bottom line? Identifying the potential of a U.S. tourism market. *Journal of Healthcare Management* 59(1) (January/February 2014):49–63.

Hussey, P. S. et al. Controlling U.S. health care spending—Separating promising from unpromising approaches. *New England Journal of Medicine* 361(22) (November 26, 2009).

Hussey, P. S., Ridgely, M. S., and Rosenthal, M. B. The PROMETHEUS bundled experiment: Slow start shows problems in implementing new payment models. *Health Affairs* 30(11) (2011):2109–2111.

Lazerow, R. *Defining Provider Risk in Accountable Payments Models.* The Advisory Board, March 2, 2011.

Miller, H. D. From volume to value: Better ways to pay for health care. *Health Affairs* 28(5) (2009):1418–1428.

Ridgely, M. S. et al. Bundled payment fails to gain a foothold in California: The experience of the IHA bundled payment demonstration. *Health Affairs* 33(8) (2014):1345–1352.

Chapter 4

CCMA: A Physician's Perspective

Sasha M. Demos

Preface

One of the, if not the most, critical components of any Clinical Co-Management Agreement (CCMA) is the role of physicians. As physicians go, so too go hospitals. Likewise, CCMAs are only as effective as physicians involved and the coordination they achieve through working in a more integrated manner. As discussed previously, CCMAs are designed to give physicians more control over service lines and the actual provision of medical services. Historically, as a consequence of specialization and the silo effect resulting from this clinical identification, physician work patterns often have reinforced a schism between physicians internally and hospitals. Few would argue that it takes a team of physicians from across specialties to effectively treat any case. But, at the same time, all are paid individually, as though each physician works in a vacuum, devoid of the interactions that are at the very essence of medicine.

Due to that seeming incongruence between the collective work of physicians and the individual payment delivery system, there has been a considerable push for reform of this system and reversal of these misaligned incentives. Governmental and private payers alike have put forth new payment systems, all in an effort to create efficiencies by the closer financial and professional alignment of physicians and hospitals. As a part of the Affordable Care Act (ACA), several different and competing methods of integrating physicians and hospitals with one another include Affordable Care Organizations (ACOs), Patient-Centered Medical Homes (PCMH), Bundled Payments, and of course, Clinical Co-Management. Other initiatives born of the ACA, such as the Medicare Center for Innovation, are seeking to overcome the initial regulatory, financial, and historical barriers to the successful implementation of a new, integrated payment model.

As such, this chapter has been authored with a firsthand perspective from a physician's point of view that recognizes both the challenges faced and the opportunities presented by Clinical Co-Management. Dr. Sasha Demos, MD, PhD, is the Chairman for the Department of Anesthesia at Edward Hospital, a large tertiary community hospital in Naperville, Illinois. Dr. Demos holds the appointment of Adjunct Professor at the University of Illinois at Chicago in the Department of Bioengineering. She received her MD from the University of Chicago and her PhD in Bioengineering from the University of Illinois at Chicago. We thank Dr. Demos for her contribution to this book and for her time in offering this unique and pragmatic view of CCMAs…

Through the eyes of a practicing physician.

Physician's Introduction

Surgical services represent one of the largest areas of costs and revenues for hospital systems nationwide. More than half of hospital expenses are spent on surgical and procedural care. With a trend toward moving surgical procedures away from hospitals and into ambulatory surgery centers, hospitals need to overhaul their surgical service lines in order to remain competitive. Keeping profit margins viable with ever-increasing costs, achieving efficiency, and providing a high-quality, safe experience are essential in achieving that goal.

Historically, hospital-based surgery has been an area that is highly fragmented with a large amount of variability. Patient satisfaction, cost, efficiency, and safety metrics, including many of the Hospital Value–Based Purchasing measures, lie within the realm of surgical care. With decreasing reimbursements, increasing costs, and the beginning of bundled payments, it is essential that hospitals find a better approach to perioperative care. The Perioperative Surgical Home (PSH), introduced by the American Society of Anesthesiologists (ASA), is one potential solution that addresses perioperative care issues (American Society of Anesthesiologists, 2011). Through the execution of CCMAs across multiple specialties and service lines, PSHs offer an exciting new integrative model.

The ASA defines the PSH as a "patient-centered and physician led multidisciplinary team based system of coordinated care that guides the patient through the entire surgical experience" (American Society of Anesthesiologists, 2011, Warner, 2012, Vetter et al., 2013). As with individual CCMAs, the goal of the wider PSH is to improve care, reduce costs, and increase patient safety and satisfaction by developing a more continuous, uniform system for perioperative medicine. Instead of fragmented surgical care that approaches the preoperative preparation of the patient, surgical and anesthesia care, and postoperative care separately, CCMAs in a PSH environment treat surgical care as a continuum, coordinating all phases of care from the decision to have surgery until 30 days post discharge. This approach aims to reduce costs, length of stay, and hospital readmissions, while improving patient satisfaction and safety.

However, there have been some financial constraints to implementing this program especially in nonacademic or non-physician-employed settings. As medicine transitions from fee-for-service to other payment models, there will be a structural gap in which payments will lag behind the change to an integrated team-based approach. Therefore, the time away from billable surgical care creates a negative financial incentive for participating physicians. However, with a collaborative system and a continuum of care, cost savings will be achieved across the entire product line. If these cost savings can be shared with all participating members, participants will be incentivized to work together as a collegial interactive team. This can be achieved through Clinical Co-Management. In this chapter, we will discuss one method of patient-centered surgical care, the PSH, and describe how Clinical Co-Management allows this program to be implemented in both academic and community medical centers.

The ASA model proposes that anesthesiologists are the ideal physicians to lead this care team for multiple reasons. First, they are experts in the area of perioperative medicine. They are already involved in preoperative testing as well as in the preoperative evaluation and medical optimization of the patients. They are also involved in the care of patients in every area of surgical care in the hospital, including all surgical subspecialties, as well as other procedural areas such as endoscopy, OB, and radiology. This results in a unique perspective on patient flow in many areas of the hospital. Postoperatively, anesthesiologists are skilled in pain management and can develop product line–specific pain management protocols. They are in a unique position to provide continuity, work with surgeons of multiple specialties, as well as nursing staff from several departments. Collaboration between multiple staff members, physicians, and administration is key to reaching these goals. Later, I will identify areas that are ripe for physician–hospital collaboration and co-management in the development of protocols and metrics to improve quality, patient satisfaction, and outcomes.

Preoperative Care

Once the decision to have surgery has been made, there are many variables that will influence a multitude of metrics further down the surgical pathway. First and foremost, the patient's medical conditions must be optimized. Healthier patients will have shorter lengths of stay, less complications, greater patient satisfaction, and lower costs than high-risk or high-acuity patients. These patients should be the most straightforward population in which to standardize care. Part of the surgical home involves preadmission testing and the presurgical medical evaluation. CCMA would allow for physicians and hospitals to work collaboratively to develop key protocols and quality metrics to be utilized in preparing patients for surgery, managing surgery, and ensuring a rapid and healthy recovery for the patient.

There are many approaches to presurgical testing and evaluation that range from a physician run preoperative clinic in which all patients are seen by an anesthesiologist prior to surgery in person, to utilization of protocols and guidelines that help determine which patients get what testing and who is informed of the information. Through CCMAs and the utilization of quality metrics, hospitals can incentivize physicians to utilize and develop such protocols to improve quality and outcome. Coordination and thoughtful evaluation of what tests are ordered can strike the balance between cost savings from preventing redundant or unnecessary testing and having enough pertinent medical information to safely continue through the surgical process from both the surgeon's and anesthesiologist's perspectives. Electronic medical records have improved access to previously performed tests and doctors' visits, while the effort of a preoperative testing program can compile copies of doctors' notes, studies, and testing to eliminate redundant tests performed based on the inability to attain prior records. By reducing unnecessary testing and streamlining care through proper quality metrics, cost savings and patient experience will be improved.

In addition to unnecessary testing, case cancellations or postponements are very costly from many perspectives. Unexpected case cancellations can be very expensive on many levels. For example, there are costs of sterile reprocessing of trays and instruments open in the operating room. Cancellations also create gaps and delays in the OR schedule which is inefficient and results in staff being paid without any incoming surgical revenue. Case cancelation can be effectively managed through physician buy-in and key metrics targeted at drivers of case cancelation.

Poor patient satisfaction can result from the inconvenience of having taken time off work, as well as having made arrangements for childcare or other personal arrangements. Additionally, patients can experience frustration from unexpected delays in care. An example of this includes being kept NPO (denied food/fluids) for a prolonged period of time or the possibility of undergoing an unpleasant intervention such as a bowel prep or radiological procedure that was intended to be timed with the cancelled procedure. As much as possible, unexpected delays or cancellations must be minimized. This can be achieved by identifying high-risk patients or patients in which their medical conditions are not optimized well in advance of surgery. This is done so that any intervention can take place prior to their scheduled surgery date or surgery rescheduled prior to arriving at the hospital. Again, through Clinical Co-Management, these interventions can be developed and properly implemented.

Preoperative testing should be organized and ordered as it relates to the procedure and the patient's medical history. Testing guidelines should be periodically reevaluated to ensure that there is not excessive testing and that the testing always reflects the current recommendations of various medical specialties. If the patient has received testing from outside facilities, every effort should be made to receive reports of these records so that redundant testing is not performed. Disease-specific protocols should be developed with input from the appropriate specialists to standardize disease-specific management and recognize medical issues that need additional attention early on. For example, a diabetes management protocol could be implemented for all diabetic patients. The protocol would establish a clear understanding regarding patient medications prior to surgery, and would assist in recognizing difficult to control diabetics. From this, intervention prior to surgery would be more feasible and would minimize surgical delays due to either uncontrolled blood sugar or patients violating their NPO status in order to correct hypoglycemia. Diabetes has been identified as an independent risk factor for postoperative morbidity, and diabetic patients can spend up to 50% more time in the hospital postoperatively compared with nondiabetic patients (Gavin, 1992, Patel and Patel, 2011). Other disease processes, such as cardiac disease, also need clear guidelines prior to surgery so that those patients that require more testing and subspecialist care are optimized without ordering unnecessary testing and consults. A process should be in place for anesthesiologists to review charts, communicate with surgeon offices, and get any testing or evaluations performed in a timely and efficient manner. By eliminating unnecessary testing, there will be less costs and inconveniences for the patients. Optimization of the patient's medical conditions before surgery will have a positive effect on the patient's intraoperative and postoperative course.

Another key area of preoperative preparation is surgical scheduling. There must be a central surgical scheduler who can coordinate the surgical cases with anesthesia availability and nurse and staff availability. An efficient schedule is to the benefit of everyone, from the hospital to the individual physicians. This scheduler should also have the ability to control other anesthetizing locations, to ensure efficiency not just in the surgical suites but in multiple areas around the hospital. There needs to be a change of thinking from individual requests and scheduling to overall institution efficiency and cost savings. An efficient schedule and proper staffing model helps prevent delays later on in the continuum of care.

Intraoperative Care

Within the OR itself, many factors contribute to the main areas of focus of a CCMA including safety, costs, efficiency, and quality. Minimizing variability within a service line helps produce consistent results at a more predictable cost. Costs can then be broken down by time, supplies and implants, staffing, and procedure type. Vendor management to unify supply purchases and reduce costs must involve input from both nursing and physicians to ensure quality and acceptable equipment at a reasonable cost. All too often, cheaper supplies are substituted without clinician input, only to result in a suboptimal product that results in clinicians using a larger quantity to get an effective result, therefore undermining any cost savings.

Alternatively, a suboptimal product may place a patient at increased risk of a medical complication, because it does not work as well as the predecessor. Surgical care requires very specific, delicate equipment in which subtle changes can have significant implications. While excessive costs must be reduced, it must never be achieved at the cost of increased risk to patients. Without a collaborative effort via a CCMA to determine from which areas cost can be cut and for which pieces of equipment can be interchanged, physicians will be frustrated and patient care can ultimately suffer.

A large area of operational costs lie in OR efficiency. A coordinated effort is necessary to achieve optimal OR efficiency. On-time starts is a basic metric that most institutions track and that requires effort from surgeons, anesthesiologists, and nursing staff to ensure that the patient is ready on time, the room is open and ready, and both physicians have seen, evaluated, and discussed the surgical or anesthetic plan with the patient. This is an easy measure to track and break down causes of delay. Causes of case delay should be tracked and the cause determined. An effective OR coordinator can be the key to identifying areas of delay and preemptively intervening before OR efficiency is affected. Any surgical delay can have a ripple effect later in the day especially if other surgeons are scheduled in the room to follow. Through a CCMA, surgical block time utilization could be carefully tracked and also both the surgeon and administration would be on the same page as to how block time is being defined. In addition, accurate and detailed data need to be made available during any discussion of inadequate block time utilization, and through standardized data collection under a CCMA, such data can be validated.

Cost needs to be looked at across the entire system, not just in individual arenas. For example, saving costs by reducing staff can have an inverse relationship to OR turnover times. Institutionally, it may be more cost effective to have more staff available to help speed turnover and improve OR efficiency even though the budget is higher for staffing. As hospitals try to keep up with the speed and efficiency of ambulatory surgery centers, they will need to invest in their staff. Hospitals are already at a structural disadvantage because the literal distance between the preoperative areas, the operating room, and the recovery rooms is greater and the normal work flow of transporting patients throughout these phases of care takes longer to maneuver. Therefore, speed must be at least competitive with ASCs in room preparation and turnover time. This is highly dependent on nurses and ancillary staff. Overworked, overstretched staff results in negative morale which does not cause people to want to work hard and work as a team to improve efficiency.

Any part of the surgical team that is noncompliant or uncooperative to the effort can undermine hard work by everyone else. That is why it is so important to change the culture to that of a collegial team with a common goal. Investing in a turnover team to assist at the start and end of various surgical cases may be worth the cost if it significantly cuts down on turnover time. In the same manner, case delays due to inpatient transport can be avoided by investing in the appropriate number of transport staff. If delays occur on weekends because there are not enough transporters, the result of delays involves significant cost, including nursing staff being paid possibly at on call or weekend rates waiting around for the patient to arrive as well as physicians waiting for the patient. More money is spent on paying the staff to wait for patients, than would be the cost of an additional transport person.

However, if cost is not looked at for the institution as a whole, but as individual budgets, these cost savings will not be realized. The cause of delays needs to be broken down and tracked to determine all areas to be addressed. Fixing one cause without addressing the others will not solve the problems. For example, if enough staff are available for room turnover, but there is an issue with central sterile processing reliability, delays will continue to occur because of instrumentation limitation. A coordinated effort must be made to identify all areas of concern and work on all simultaneously in order to see the largest improvements.

All efforts towards efficiency though must never be achieved at the cost or risk of safety. Any time there is a question of patient concern, the entire team must not feel pressured to get the patient in the room without having necessary lab tests or adequate time to talk to the patient. In this day and age of improving efficiency, physicians are often pressured to have hurried discussions with the patient and their family, or not wait for the family to arrive, separate the patient from their family due to flow issues, etc., in order to achieve the goal of on-time starts. Establishing and maintaining a strong patient–doctor relationship involves having time to reassure and answer any questions the patient or family member may have. Often it has been told to physicians that they have already spoken to the patient in the office so not much time is needed pre-procedure. Many patients now have family members with them who may have questions or need additional reassurance. Also, patients are most likely meeting their anesthesiologist for the first time so the few minutes prior to surgery are the only time available to meet and develop a rapport with that patient.

These discussions between physicians and patients should not be rushed. Patients sometimes do not arrive at the hospital as early as they are requested so there is very little time between preparing the patient for their procedure and that procedure's scheduled start time. Due to the pressure on physicians to have on-time starts and the tracking of late starts, this patient–physician interaction is hastened. We need to keep track of the big picture and the best interest of the patient. In a CCMA, efficiency is an important metric and can assist in cost savings, but, I must emphasize again, under no circumstances should efficiency be gained at the expense of the patient safety or the doctor–patient relationship. Patient satisfaction is a critical dimension of care, and it is also a key part of value-based purchasing metrics.

Furthermore, medical liability can be an enormous cost to the health system. Studies repeatedly show that the patients are much less likely to sue their doctor if they have a good relationship with them. In a 1997 study, Dr. Wendy Levinson of the University of Toronto reviewed hundreds of conversations between physicians and patients. She then divided the doctors into two groups, half of the doctors had never been sued, while the other half had been sued at least twice. Of the doctors that had never been sued, those doctors spent more than 3 min longer with each patient than did those who had been sued (18.3 vs. 15 min, respectively). They also were more likely to engage in active listening, more likely to include comments regarding listening such as, "I will leave time for your questions" and more likely to laugh. There was no difference in the quality or quantity of information doctors gave (Levinson et al., 1997). This serves to emphasize the benefit of patient–physician communication.

The use of evidence-based practices will also assist in providing the best patient outcomes. This has been demonstrated with Enhanced Recovery after Surgery (ERAS) protocols and other fast track evidence-based protocols (Zhuang et al., 2013). ERAS protocols are multimodal perioperative care pathways. The goals are to attenuate the surgical stress response, minimize postoperative pain, and reduce complications. As these programs become more widespread, many studies show that they are a safe and effective way to reduce hospital stay without increasing readmissions (Aarts et al., 2012, Paton et al., 2014). These protocols are developed for specific surgical procedures using evidence-based practices across the continuum of care. Through a CCMA, these protocols can be further developed and implemented through collaboration between physicians and the hospital administration, and both parties, as well as patients, will realize significantly improved outcomes.

Postoperative Care

Coordinating postoperative care and identifying areas of risk are essential to providing optimal care to the patient. Minimizing complications and decreasing the length of stay improve patient satisfaction, reduce costs, and improve the quality of care. As much as patient's variable medical history allows, postoperative protocols should be in place to standardize care. Areas that affect postoperative care can be broken down into those that affect recovery and patient satisfaction, such as postoperative nausea and vomiting prevention and pain controls, those that affect specific patient medical issues, such as diabetes and sleep apnea management, those that affect mobility, such as physical therapy, and other factors that can affect discharge such as social services.

One of the most common side effects of anesthesia is postoperative nausea and vomiting (PONV). In terms of patient satisfaction, nausea, pain, and vomiting rank among the highest concerns in the immediate postoperative period. Many studies have shown that patients find PONV even more distressing than pain (Gan et al., 2001, Van den Bosch et al., 2006). In addition to being unpleasant, PONV also can have significant medical consequences, including dehydration, wound dehiscence, hematoma formation near surgical sites, aspiration if airway reflexes are decreased or if the patient underwent facial or jaw surgery. PONV can prolong time in the recovery unit and accounts for 0.1%–0.2% of unanticipated hospital admissions (Smith et al., 2012) which contributes to increased costs. Approximately, 30% of all patients experience PONV, although the rate varies with the number of risk factors. Even patients with no risk factors experience PONV 10% of the time and the incidence can reach 60%–80% in patients with multiple risk factors (Gan et al., 2003, Smith et al., 2012). Although multiple studies looking at a variety of antiemetics have revealed that at this time there is no way to eliminate PONV, the use of risk stratification tools and treatment protocols or guidelines can assist in reducing the incidence of this negative side effect thereby improving patient satisfactions, minimizing associated complications, and reducing costs.

The next largest area affecting patient satisfaction is pain control. Inadequate pain control contributes not only to a negative patient experience but also to physiological changes such as increased heart rate and blood pressure that can have further consequences and lead to increased perioperative morbidity. Uncontrolled pain can result in longer PACU stays, longer hospital stays, and prevent early ambulation and motility which is necessary to minimize other complications such as blood clots and risk of pulmonary embolism. Postoperative pulmonary morbidity can also be increased if the patient is not able to take deep breaths secondary to incisional or surgical pain. Some patients may not be able to complete required physical therapy if their pain is not adequately controlled.

Pain control management can begin as early as the preoperative period with setting proper expectations. Patients need to understand that depending on the procedure or surgery, they will experience some pain and discomfort. However, every effort will be made to manage excessive pain. Since pain medications themselves have inherent risks and side effects, such as nausea, constipations, and respiratory depressions, setting proper expectations will help prevent unexpected delays in discharge or unexpected admissions. For specific surgical procedures, pain protocols can be developed using a multimodal approach including both narcotic and non-narcotic pain medications, local anesthetics, regionals, and neuraxial anesthesia approaches when applicable. Evidence-based practices and procedure-specific pain protocols can reduce variability and help to ensure proper pain control.

Utilization of ancillary services should be considered when developing the patient pathway. Protocols and consistent care for surgical service lines need to be in place with regard to physical therapy or other applicable ancillary services. Consistency will be achieved if patients within a service line are receiving a known treatment plan. The best example of this would be with total joint patients. There should not be an effect on length of stay whether the surgery is performed on Monday or Friday. However, availability and coordination of ancillary services on the weekend will be essential to ensure there is no delay in discharge or an effect on recovery due to decreased physical therapy staff or social work staff. Set protocols provide more consistent, better quality care for all the patients.

One area of significant cost to hospitals is that of readmission within 30 days of discharge. In order to prevent unexpected hospital readmissions, high-risk patients must be identified and an early intervention protocol in place prior to readmissions. Diligent follow-up care must be provided and detailed postoperative instructions given. For patients in which language or cultural barriers exist, proper resources must be allocated to ensure understanding and improve chances for compliance. Investment in a liaison or patient coordinator that can follow up with high-risk patients, help them self-monitor, and catch problems or symptoms before they become severe will help minimize the risk of readmission. Through Clinical Co-Management, a system can be developed so that even prior to surgery the expectations and means for communication postoperatively are fully explained to the patient. The patient needs to understand what to be on the watch for, who to call, and how to ask questions whether daytime, evening, or weekend so that complications and medical issues can be caught early and managed as an outpatient, rather than worsening at home and the patient coming to the ER.

Clinical Co-Management as the Solution to Implementation

Clinical Co-Management can be used as a mechanism to bring together physicians and the hospital to reach their common goals of decreasing costs, improving safety and quality, and increasing patient satisfaction. For surgical service lines, engaging both anesthesiologists and surgeons is essential to optimizing outcomes. Establishing CCMAs changes the historically fragmented surgical care model into a patient-centered continuous one. As discussed, portions of the surgical care cannot be viewed in compartments. In doing so, cost saving in one area may actually lead to increased costs overall. For example, the decision to not perform a peripheral nerve block for an orthopedic case in order to save a few minutes of time may result in increased pain and a prolonged PACU stay or even an unexpected hospital readmission for pain control. By looking at what is in the best interest of the patient overall, decisions can be made in more of a global manner that will improve overall care. In this chapter, for simplicity's sake, the surgical process was divided into three distinct parts, preoperative, intraoperative, and postoperative; but in reality each part is deeply connected to one another. The chapter has highlighted dozens of areas of opportunity for collaboration between multiple physician specialties and hospital administration, but due to the complexity of the clinical relationships and the void of appropriate incentive, these opportunities are best realized through CCMA. A CCMA would unite physicians and hospital administration to common, agreed upon, protocols, metrics, and goals that will improve quality of care, patient satisfaction, and care efficiency while sharing financial incentives between both collaborating parties.

The PSH concept addressed these issues by applying best practices and setting up a system that considers the entire surgical experience of the patient. By implementing this concept practically with a Clinical Co-Management structure, all participating members have a vested interest in achieving the global goals, and not just benefiting individual physicians or phases of care. Most surgical Clinical Co-Management contracts have been written between the hospital and the surgeons. These contracts address many aspects of surgical care, although they often just focus on the intraoperative period. By including anesthesiologists, surgeons, and hospital administration, an all-encompassing approach to the entire continuum of surgical care can be achieved, maximizing cost savings, creating the highest level of quality and safety, and optimizing patient satisfaction. The co-management contracts incentivize all involved to direct their efforts to create and implement a patient-centered surgical environment, as well as provide a structure to monitor, track, and continue to make adjustments to improve their outcomes.

References

Aarts, M. A., Okrainec, A., Glicksman, A., Pearsall, E., Victor, J. C., and McLeod, R. S. Adoption of enhanced recovery after surgery (ERAS) strategies for colorectal surgery at academic teaching hospitals and impact on total length of hospital stay. *Surgical Endoscopy* 26(2) (February 2012):442–450.

American Society of Anesthesiologists. *The Perioperative of Surgical Home*. American Society of Anesthesiologists, Washington, DC, 2011.

Gan, T. J., Meyer, T., Apfel, C. C. et al. Consensus guidelines for managing postoperative nausea and vomiting. *Anesthesia & Analgesia* 97 (2003):62–71.

Gan, T., Sloan, F., Dear Gde, L. et al. How much are patients willing to pay to avoid postoperative nausea and vomiting? *Anesthesia & Analgesia* 92 (2001):393–400.

Gavin, L. A. Review: Perioperative management of the diabetic patient. *Endocrinology & Metabolism Clinics of North America* 21(2) (June 1992):457–475.

Levinson, W., Roter, D. L., Mullooly, J. P., Dull, V. T., and Frankel, R. M. Physician—Patient communication: The relationship with malpractice claims among primary care physicians and surgeons. *JAMA* 277(7) (1997):553–559.

Patel, N. M. and Patel, M. S. Medical complications of obesity and optimization of the obese patient for colorectal surgery. *Clinics in Colon & Rectal Surgery* 24(4) (December 2011):211–221.

Paton, F., Chambers, D., Wilson, P., Eastwood, A., Craig, D., Fox, D., Jayne, D., and McGinnes, E. Effectiveness and implementation of enhanced recovery after surgery programmes: A rapid evidence synthesis. *BMJ Open* 4 (2014):e005015.

Smith, H. S, Smith, E. J., and Smith, B. R. Postoperative nausea and vomiting. *Annals of Palliative Medicine* 1 (2012):94–102.

Van den Bosch, J. E., Bonsel, G. J., Moons, K. G. et al. Effect of postoperative experiences on willingness to pay to avoid postoperative pain, nausea, and vomiting. *Anesthesiology* 104 (2006):1033–1039.

Vetter, T. R., Goeddel, L. A., Boudreaux, A. M., Hunt, T. R., Jones, K. A., and Pittet, J. F. The perioperative surgical home: How can it make the case so everyone wins? *BMC Anesthesiology* 13 (2013):6.

Warner, M. A. The surgical home. *ASA Newsletter* 76(5) (2012):30–32.

Zhuang, C. L., Ye, X. Z., Zhang, X. D., Chen, B. C., and Yu, Z. Enhanced recovery after surgery programs versus traditional care for colorectal surgery: A meta-analysis of randomized controlled trials. *Diseases of the Colon & Rectum* 56(5) (May 2013):667–678.

Chapter 5

Regulatory Compliance

Having now provided the historical background that has brought the healthcare system to its current point, a roadmap of where the system is headed, and an on-the-ground perspective, we now delve into the nuts-and-bolts sections of constructing and maintaining a Clinical Co-Management Agreement (CCMA). This chapter will focus on the regulatory and administrative framework under which an effective and compliant CCMA is developed.

CCMAs can be difficult to implement due to numerous regulatory concerns. This chapter should serve as a guide when navigating the potential pitfalls in designing and implementing a CCMA. The chapter will address the legal considerations and policy concerns that impact a CCMA.

Legal Considerations

Although not part of a coherent, coordinated framework, a CCMA must be compliant with the patchwork of fraud and abuse laws and regulations, to avoid indirect implication resulting in sanction. The federal fraud and abuse laws include the Ethics in Patient Referrals Act* (Stark Law), the Anti-Kickback Statute,† and the Civil Monetary Penalties Law‡ (CMP). The risk of sanction under these regulatory schemes is exacerbated by the fact that neither CMS, the enforcement agency behind the Stark Law, nor the OIG, the enforcement agency behind the AKS and CMP, has published definitive guidelines on how CCMAs should be structured. Each respective law including the legal framework, examples related to a CCMA, safeguards as put forth to provide guidance when developing a CCMA, and applicability upon the development of a CCMA is outlined next. Each law must be carefully considered when drafting a CCMA and common questions need to be asked to ensure continued legality.

Stark Law

> Does the CCMA create a financial relationship between the hospital and participating physicians? Does the CCMA cover the provision of designated health services?

The Stark Law prohibits physicians from referring Medicare and Medicaid patients to any entity with which the physician (or an immediate family member) has a financial relationship for the provision of designated health services,§ unless an

* 42 U.S.C. § 1395nn et seq.; 42 C.F.R. § 411.350 et seq.

† 42 U.S.C. § 1320a-7b(b); 42 C.F.R. § 1001.952 et seq.

‡ 42 U.S.C. § 1320a-7(b)(1)-(2); 42 C.F.R. § 1003.100 et seq.

§ 42 C.F.R. §§ 411.350–411.389; Designated health services include the following: clinical laboratory services, physical therapy, occupational therapy and speech-language pathology services, radiology and certain other imaging services, radiation therapy services and supplies, durable medical equipment and supplies, parental and enteral nutrients, equipment and supplies, prosthetics, orthotics and prosthetic devices and supplies, home health services, outpatient prescription drugs, and inpatient and outpatient hospital services.42 C.F.R. § 411.351.

exception applies. As an example, Physician A cannot refer a patient to Hospital A if Physician A has a financial relationship (e.g. employment, ownership, management) with Hospital A, unless the relationship falls in a Stark exception.

The Stark Law is a strict liability statute that results in liability if a physician fails to meet an exception. Although existing Stark exceptions are potentially applicable to CCMAs, CMS published a proposed Stark exception that provides increased guidance. The proposed exception would require the following:

- Duration of agreement for a term of at least 1 year and no more than 3 years
- Participation by a group of at least five physicians
- Open to all medical staff members in the particular specialty
- Restricted only to those on the medical staff at commencement of the program
- Objective measurements for changes in quality—ideally quality measures derived from CMS National Quality Measures
- Performance measures supported by independent evidence demonstrating that the measures would not adversely impact patient care
- Performance measures must reasonably relate to the hospital's practice and population
- Performance measure baselines should be adjusted annually
- Maintaining a performance without improvement should not be rewarded—actual improvement from baseline is necessary
- Payment by hospital to Physician Management Company (PMC) on an aggregate basis
- Payment by physician group to each physician on per capita basis
- Payments must be specific to satisfaction of each measure

- Payments are monetary in nature—not other types of incentives (e.g. equipment, reduced rent)
- Payments tied to quality and efficiency should be capped at 50% of cost savings
- Payments should not be based on a reduction in the length of stay for a particular patient or hospital operations in the aggregate
- Independent reviewer/auditor to review program prior to commencement and annually
- Written notice to patient prior to procedure*

Compensation for management services creates a financial relationship, so the CCMA must fall within a Stark exception, otherwise their referrals to the hospital could be viewed as suspect. The key goals of the proposed exception are transparency, quality, and ensuring there are proper protections to prevent the possibility of payment for patient referrals. Hospitals and physicians can avoid federal scrutiny by keeping these goals in mind and complying with the aforementioned guidance.

Anti-Kickback Statute

> Is the CCMA intended to disguise remuneration from the hospital to reward or induce referrals by the participating physicians?

According to the Anti-Kickback Statute, it is illegal to offer, pay, solicit, or receive remuneration to *induce or reward referrals* of items or services reimbursable in whole or in part by federal or state healthcare programs.† As an example, Hospital A cannot give a physician money or anything of value

* Shared Savings Exception, 73 Fed. Reg. 38502, 38553 (proposed July 7, 2008) (to be codified at 42 § 411.357(x)).

† 42 U.S.C. § 1320a-7b.

(e.g. free use of space) in exchange for the physician agreeing to refer patients to Hospital A.

This statute is an intent-based, criminal liability statute. Numerous safe harbors, if met, protect criminal (and civil) exposure under the statute. Failure to meet a safe harbor does not, however, indicate liability under the statute. The OIG recognizes several safeguards in advisory opinions, including

- Written agreement limited to a 3-year term
- Performance payments subject to an annual cap, which ensures an increase in patient referrals will not result in increased physician compensation
- Participation open to all physicians who have been on staff for at least 1 year, and not just high-referring physicians
- Performance compensation does not depend on, or vary with, number of patients treated; compensation is paid at fair market value
- Distribution to participating physicians is made *per capita*,* which reduces risk of rewarding individual physicians for increased referrals
- Performance measures are specific and supported by credible medical evidence, so as to ensure intent to improve the quality of care rather than reward referrals
- Patients receive notice of the agreement prior to receiving services†

Compensation from CCMAs for management services and meeting certain benchmarks triggers the law because, if structured incorrectly, a CCMA could appear to be a mechanism to pay for referrals under the Anti-Kickback Statute.

* Office of Inspector Gen., Dep't of Health & Human Services, Advisory Op. 12-22 (December 31, 2012) [hereinafter Advisory Op. 12-22].

† Office of Inspector Gen., Dep't of Health & Human Services, Advisory Op. 08-16 (October 7, 2008) [hereinafter Advisory Op. 08-16]; Advisory Op. 12-22.

Civil Monetary Penalties Law

> Does the Agreement induce participating physicians to reduce or limit services provided to patients?

The CMP Law prohibits arrangements that provide physicians with incentives to reduce or limit items or services to patients that are under clinical care. As an example, Hospital A cannot give a physician money or anything of value in exchange for the physician providing less care to patients. It is important to keep in mind that the law applies to both direct and indirect arrangements that could lead to incentivizing reduced care.

Some CCMAs provide compensation to physicians in exchange for reducing costs in a number of areas (e.g. limiting unnecessary use of supplies, utilizing less expensive equipment or drugs). There are no bright-line exceptions or safe harbors under the CMP Law, which increases both uncertainty and risk for arrangements like CCMAs. However, the OIG recognizes several safeguards in advisory opinions, including

- Agreement reasonably limited in duration, with a maximum 3-year term
- Performance payments reasonably limited in amount, with a set maximum annual cap
- Performance measures supported by credible medical evidence and reasonably relate to the hospital's practice
- Performance compensation not reduced if a specific performance measure is contraindicated with a specific patient's care
- Annual independent, third-party valuation of the fair market value of both the fixed management fee and the performance fee
- Annual internal and independent, third-party audits of performance measures, resulting in written findings and certification of no adverse effect on patient care

- Continuous monitoring of the agreement's effect on physician referral practices, and if any participating physician's practice changes significantly, due in any part to the performance incentives, the physician should be terminated
- Agreement prohibits doctors from
  - Limiting usage of quality improving but more costly devices, tests or treatments ("stinting")
  - Treating only healthier patients ("cherry picking")
  - Avoiding sicker patients and steering healthier patients to the hospital ("steering")
  - Discharging patients earlier to home or post-acute care settings ("quicker-sicker discharge")
- Patients receive notice of the agreement prior to receiving any services

Some CCMAs provide compensation to physicians in exchange for reducing costs in a number of areas (e.g. limiting unnecessary use of supplies, utilizing less expensive equipment or drugs). The CMP Law places heavy scrutiny on these arrangements because of potential reduction of services at the risk of patient health in order to increase incentive compensation.

Policy Concerns Underlying Fraud and Abuse Laws

With regard to the Anti-Kickback Statute and CMP Law, the OIG historically focuses on three policy aspects: (1) accountability, (2) quality controls, and (3) safeguards against payments for referrals.* CMS, with regard to the Stark Law, aims to protect against "sham" agreements, which use illegitimate

* Statement of Lewis Morris, Chief Counsel to the Inspector General, Office of Inspector General, U.S. Department of Health and Human Services, Hearing on Gainsharing, Committee on Ways and Means, U.S. House of Representatives, 109th Congress, October 7, 2005. *See also*, Fed. Reg., April 30, 2008 at 23693.

performance measures designed in substance to reward physicians for referrals rather than the achievement of legitimate benchmarks for quality maintenance or cost savings. Underlying all of these regulations are six main policy concerns: unfair competition, payments for referrals, cherry picking, steering, quicker-sicker discharge, and stinting. The first five policy concerns involve agreements that incentivize physician action, while the last policy concern involves agreements that limit physician action.

Unfair competition results when an agreement serves as an inducement to attract physicians from competing hospitals, or gain physician loyalty with the intent to gain referrals. A further instance of unlawful referrals, called payment for referrals, results when an agreement may in form look like a compliant CCMA designed to meet quality care or cost-saving benchmarks, while in substance it rewards physicians for referrals to the hospital.

There are also policy concerns involving incentives based on patient care and how these patients are cared for. Cherry picking results when an agreement provides incentives for physicians to selectively treat only healthier, and less costly, patients, in order to meet performance benchmarks. Steering results when an agreement provides incentives for physicians to select only healthier patients and refer these patients to the hospital, to assist in meeting performance benchmarks. Quicker-sicker discharge results when an agreement may provide incentives for physicians to discharge patients earlier than prior to the implementation of the agreement, resulting in an adverse effect on quality of care.

There is a policy concern that impedes a physician decisions in individual patient care. Stinting results when an agreement may limit the discretion of physicians to make medically appropriate decisions for their patients, including, but not limited to, decisions about tests, treatments, procedures, services, supplies or discharge, which may result in reductions or limitations in patient care.

CMS also expressed concerns regarding the number of participating physicians under a co-management agreement, suggesting programs should only be offered to "pools" of "five or more" physicians.* This suggestion corresponds to the definition of a "group practice" under the Stark Law with regard to payment of productivity bonuses and profit shares.† When confronted with commenters requesting a reduction in the required number of participating physicians, CMS replied:

> We believe a threshold of at least five physicians is likely to be broad enough to attenuate the ties between compensation and referrals. We are rejecting the suggestion to use a threshold of three physicians because we believe that the lesser threshold would result in pooling that would be too narrow and, therefore, potentially too closely related to DHS referrals.‡

CMS, therefore, has shown reluctance to allow fewer than five physicians to participate in bonus/incentive programs, voicing concerns as to violations of the Stark law.§ However, when formulating the previously proposed Stark exception for incentive programs, CMS specifically solicited comments on the matter:

> We are interested in comments about our proposal to require hospitals to create pools for purposes of physician participation in incentive payment and shared savings programs and the minimum number of physicians needed to comprise a 'pool' that adequately reduces the risk of program or

* 73 Fed. Reg. at 38554.

† 66 Fed. Reg. 856, 909 (proposed January 4, 2001); 42 C.F.R. § 411.352(i)(2)-(3).

‡ 66 Fed. Reg. at 909.

§ *See* 42 C.F.R. § 411.352(i)(2)-(3) (incorporating the "five or more" rule into the final regulation).

> patient abuse.... Specifically, we are interested in comments on whether and, if so, how we should address the 'pooling' of funds for payment purposes in an incentive payment or shared savings program targeted at a specific medical specialty or hospital department in which the physicians on the medical staff in that specialty or department or in the physician organization total fewer than five physicians. *

In the same vein, CMS solicited comments regarding alternative approaches to the proposed *per capita* distribution requirement:

> We are interested in public comments that may outline alternate approaches to the *per capita* payment model for the distribution of incentive payments or shared savings payments, such as paying a physician more or less according to whether he or she contributed more or less to the achievement of the performance measures included in the incentive payment or shared savings program.†

Although no further instruction has been provided by CMS, these comment solicitations demonstrate an awareness by the department that there is not a one-size fits all solution for all CCMAs, and alternative approaches may be required in certain situations.

Having provided an explanation of the legal pitfalls and policy concerns in play with regard to CCMA, the following chapter will explain how to work within this legal framework to establish a well-structured and compliant CCMA.

---

* 73 Fed. Reg. at 38554.

† *Id.* at 38555.

Chapter 6

Implementation

Now, having provided an explanation of the legal and regulatory considerations surrounding Clinical Co-Management Agreements (CCMAs), we will examine the steps to implementation.

The first step in a successful CCMA is determining and defining the scope of the CCMA. Once the scope is defined, the legal structure of the physician–hospital relationship must be considered and developed. Following the legal structure, the general compensation model and terms are negotiated and established. Having established general compensation terms, data collection begins and key responsibilities and metrics are identified and refined for use as a part of the incentive compensation. Once data have been collected and metrics are identified, the proposed agreement is provided to a third-party valuation company to determine the fair market value of the incentive payments tied to the performance metrics. Once valued, the CCMA goes into effect, but data are continuously collected to track performance and other potential metrics are identified for implementation in later years.

Determine the Scope

You must first successfully define the scope in order to ensure a successful CCMA. The scope includes things like the service line, inpatient or outpatient, the specialties that will be included in the agreement, if only specific facilities will be covered, and the types of services the physicians will manage or impact through their action driven by the CCMA.

In order to effectively define the scope, the hospital and key physicians should work collectively to evaluate what the current needs exist that could be addressed via co-management. The hospital administration, with input from physicians, should perform an analysis designed to evaluate current performance and identify areas ripe for improvement. Physician input is key because an in-depth understanding of the subject matter may be necessary to identify opportunities for improvement. Other potential sources for the identification of opportunities for improvement include internal quality reports, external reports, and patient satisfaction surveys. If the hospital's internal database is not sufficient to meet the needs of the quality assessment, there are many external databases that can be accessed to identify areas for improvement.

After hospital administration has worked with physicians and reviewed internal and external information to identify broad areas of need, the hospital can then define the scope of the CCMA. The scope will act as the base for the future structure of the CCMA, and once it is developed the next step is determining what structure the CCMA will take.

Legal Structure of the CCMA

There are several options that should be considered when selecting the CCMA structure to be utilized in contracting between the physicians and the hospital. The most common structures are the hospital directly contracting with the physicians, the hospital contracting with a physician-owned management company, or the hospital contracting with a jointly owned management company in which the hospital and physicians each maintain ownership.

Under the direct contract structure, physicians (or potentially a physician group) directly enter into a contract with the hospital to provide the co-management services. There is no additional entity created in this structure, and physicians (or the physician group) are a direct party to the contract with the hospital. Under this structure, a management council is created and the council comprises both hospital administration and the physicians that are directly party to the agreement. The council is responsible for implementing and effectuating solutions to reach the goals of the CCMA. This structure has limited efficacy as it requires direct contracting with individual physicians (or physician groups), which could limit the scope of the CCMA. See Figure 6.1 for the depiction of the arrangement.

In order to address this shortfall present in the direct contracting structure, there is the physician-owned management company structure. Under this structure, a separate entity, a physician management company (PMC) is incorporated (often a limited liability company, or LLC, for favorable tax treatment and reduced liability) by the physicians. The physicians taking

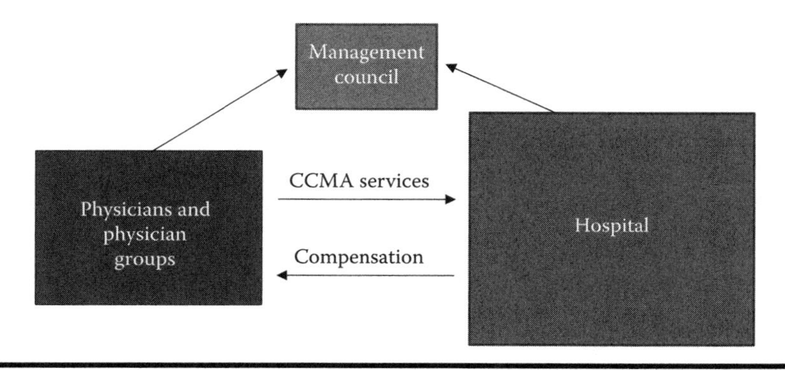

Figure 6.1 Direct CCMA structure.

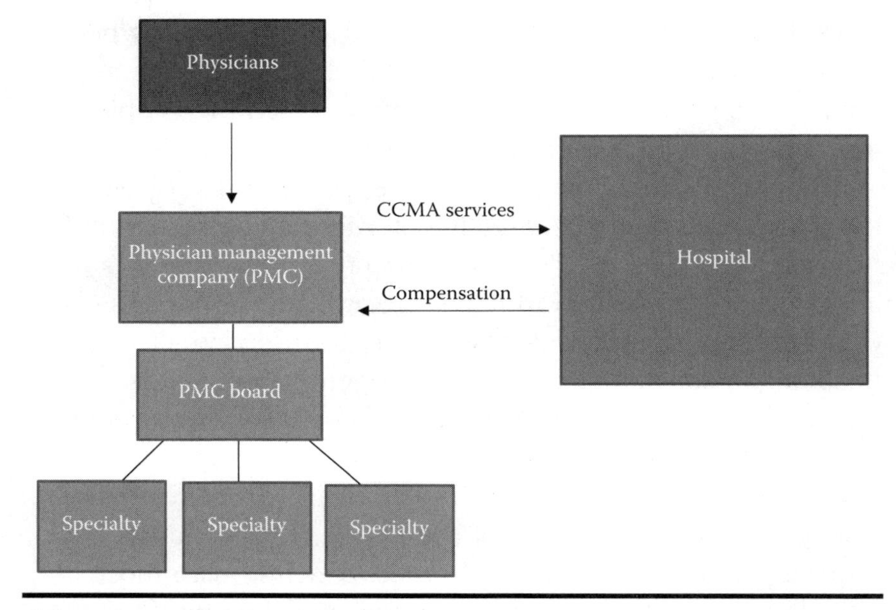

Figure 6.2 PMC CCMA structure.

part in the CCMA join the PMC as members/owners. The PMC then contracts with the hospital to provide the services required by the CCMA. This PMC structure is ideal because it is flexible and capable of addressing varying scopes within CCMAs and for the favorable legal protections afforded to the physicians via a corporate entity. For example, if the CCMA includes multiple specialties, the PMC would be able to create committees within itself responsive to the different unique services that the specialties are responsible for. See Figure 6.2 for depiction of the arrangement.

A variant of the PMC Structure is the Joint Venture Management Company (JVMC) Structure. As the name suggests, this structure allows for both the physicians and the hospital to share joint interests in the management company. This structure may be preferable in situations where the hospital administration desires closer ties to the management company and desires to play a bigger role in shaping the implementation of the CCMA.

There are both potential advantages and disadvantages in pursuing a JVMC. One significant benefit of a JVMC is the ability for the JVMC to have access to the support of the hospital's in-house resources necessary to operate a corporate entity. Potential resources the hospital could provide to the JVMC are legal services, accounting, finance, and other back-office functions. However, at the same time physicians may perceive a hospital wanting to have control of the JVMC as a lack of confidence in the physicians, and that could undermine the physicians' motivation to take part in co-management of the service. One of the goals of a CCMA is to place more power and responsibility in their hands of physicians. If physicians believe a hospital is actually trying to limit the management and oversight of the physicians, via attempting to control the JVMC, then the entire CCMA could be undermined. Thus, while a JVMC structure may be the most ideal, it is also the most complicated and should be thoroughly vetted. See Figure 6.3 for depiction of the arrangement.

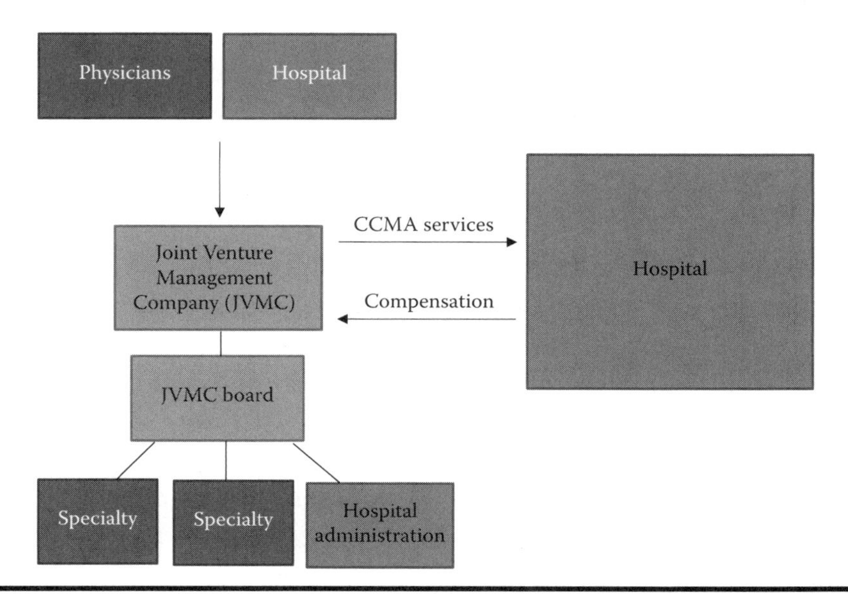

Figure 6.3 JVMC CCMA structure.

While this section provides a general overview of the pros and cons of the three structural options, Direct, PMC, and JVMC, hospital administration and physicians should keep in mind that each agreement will have unique goals and challenges, and there are more complex administrative and legal considerations to weigh that will be unique to each organization and agreement. For those reasons, when identifying what structure to use, it is imperative to weigh all of the options thoroughly and seek legal and operational expertise to ensure success. After identifying the organizational structure, parties must next consider a viable compensation structure.

Administrative Structure

As we have seen in Figures 6.1 through 6.3, CCMAs are tied together by some type of Joint Council/Board which creates a forum for physicians and hospitals to work in a collaborative, scheduled manner. Too often, in the absence of an overarching board to mediate and to solve problems, the process is completely ad hoc, with physicians and hospital administrators reacting to situations and bouncing back and forth from emergency to emergency as they arise. Joint Councils change this paradigm, in which issues are put on a schedule and dealt with in a timely, efficient manner. This serves several important purposes. First, by being a neutral background set up for exchange and information and filled with physicians and administrators alike, a Joint Council seeks to establish a nondefensive atmosphere conducive to engagement and resolution. Second, by creating this environment, Joint Councils allow the parties involved to move away from simply being problem identifiers and move them toward being problem solvers. Interaction with and within the Joint Council will only strengthen over the course of the CCMA too as responsibilities are defined and as the Joint Council's authority matures. For the first year of the CCMA, monthly Joint Council meetings are recommended, but subsequently, in most cases, it will be appropriate to move to quarterly meetings.

Compensation Structure

Defining the compensation structure can be challenging due how heavily regulated the healthcare industry is. Due to the laws and regulations discussed earlier, hospitals and physicians must take great care in how the compensation of a CCMA is designed. For this reason, hospitals and physicians should educate themselves or seek expertise early in the process in order to begin on the right path and avoid potential pitfalls. With that in mind, two broad categories of compensation structure, base compensation and incentive compensation, are discussed later.

Base Compensation

In return for the management/administrative services provided by the physicians, the hospital agrees to pay the management company a base fee. The base fee is generally in the form of either hourly compensation paid on the basis of documented time spent by the physicians providing base services or a fixed rate for a defined period of time (e.g. annual fee). Of the two options, an hourly rate base fee is preferable because it presents less risk with regard to potential for running afoul against compensation restrictions in place due to the applicable laws and regulations. With documented time spent performing specific activities, hospitals are able to validate the compensation and avoid any allegations of overcompensation that could occur when a flat fee is paid.

Table 6.1 Potential CCMA Base Services

• Direct day-to-day management • Development of service line • Develop/implement strategic plan • Provide clinical education • Medical director services • Assure appropriate professional staffing • Develop clinical protocols/ performance standards • Direct, oversee, and participate in quality assurance • Identify best practices per service line	• Implement programs to reduce adverse effects • Develop and implement patient care policies • Improve productivity of service line • Ongoing assessment of clinical environment and work flow processes • Assure adequate scheduling of physician

Base services are those services that the management company, via the physicians, performs in return for payment of the base fee. The services performed will be very dependent on the needs of the hospital. Some potential services are outlined in Table 6.1.

The degree of physician engagement is directly impacted by the number of base services included in the contract. The greater number of items identified earlier included in the agreement the greater level of engagement from the physicians. By providing broad co-management authority, the hospital empowers the physicians to facilitate change in the service line's performance.

Incentive Compensation

The incentive payment is the second fee component that may be included in a CCMA. Incentive payments differ from base fees as the charges are not attached to hourly based services provided by the co-management company. Instead, the co-manager receives compensation if, at the end of the applicable measuring period, the co-management company meets or exceeds a number of predetermined performance metrics or goals. Thus, the incentive payment focuses on significant accomplishments of the co-manager in contrast to hourly based services.

Incentive payments must be assessed at fair market value and cannot be designed to induce co-management referrals. Acceptable incentive payment components may include achievement of quality goals, operational efficiency goals that do not result in the reduction of care to patients, patient/staff satisfaction goals, and new program development. Gainsharing measures can be acceptable despite a heightened risk under current law. This time of arrangement would encourage physicians to identify efficiency opportunities and then share in a percentage of the realized savings that would result from the reduction in the overall cost of providing the patient care.

This type of arrangement is most often seen in surgical services that experience high costs in the form of equipment and supplies. For example, there could be a metric that incentivized surgeons to reduce the overall cost of the episode of care and the surgeon could achieve that by identifying protocols to more efficiently utilize supplies. However, it is important to keep in mind that any type of metric tracking cost savings should ensure it does not impact patient care. Additionally, although time consuming and costly, it is advisable to obtain OIG approval of specific measures prior to implementing strategies that involve shared savings of direct costs as advisory opinions issued by the OIG have resulted in narrow findings.

As has been discussed throughout this book, verifiable and validated data are key for effective incentive metrics. For this reason, the data collection phase of CCMAs is often a significant boon to the hospitals and physicians in ways they would not have anticipated. During the data collection process, hospitals and physicians will find themselves having a more open dialogue regarding strategies and goals, and, while the process may be challenging, ultimately it will lead to each group having a better understanding of the strengths and weaknesses that exist within the service. Oftentimes, the data collection and review lead to the identification of gaps that neither party was aware of but both want to address.

Metrics and Data

Incentivizing performance must be tied to real and verifiable improvements in a particular service line or the facility at large.* It is not sufficient to simply claim that a CCMA is going to be used to align physicians with the hospital or that it will improve relationships with physicians in the community; federal regulatory standards directly prohibit these actions.† From this need for a real and verifiable means to show improvements, data and metrics become the real heart of any CCMA.

To give an idea of what type of data is necessary for defining metrics, here are examples of potential CCMA metrics:

Operational

- Surgical on-time starts
- Operating room turnaround time
- Block utilization rates
- Adherence to supply preference cards
- Delay reduction
- Diagnostic test turnaround times
- Supply cost per case
- Physician consultation timeliness

Qualitative

- Compliance with national quality measures (SCIP, AMI, HF, NHQM)
- Infection rates

* Shared savings exception, 73 Fed. Reg. 38502, at 38553.

† 42 U.S.C. § 1320a-7b (2010); 42 C.F.R. §§ 411.350–411.389 (2010).

- Mortality rates
- Medication reconciliation
- Proper and timely medication administration
- Readmission rates

Satisfaction

- Patient satisfaction rates (both internal and HCAHPS)
- Staff satisfaction

New initiative development

- Development of Community Outreach and Education Initiative
- Development of Clinical Affiliation Network

Metrics not only show performance as benchmarked against national, accredited standards, but also over time, as service lines and facilities develop. Data become the only source of verifiable trust designed to satisfy regulatory standards as well as to build rapport and coordination of care within the service line or hospital. Absent that real, identifiable substance, the Office of the Inspector General (OIG) may interpret the CCMA as improper under the federal Stark Law, the Anti-Kickback Statute, and other regulations, thereby resulting in significant liability. Thus, building clear support for arrangements through the use of data is essential.

Unfortunately, one of the biggest challenges in CCMA design and implementation revolves around that data. During that process, it is common that when providers assess their baseline data, they find that the overall efficacy of existing data is lacking. Provider's data may be too general in scope to meet the specific needs that exist. Furthermore, data may not be organized in a way that facilitates review of targeted work, for example by service line or physician. Hospitals often discover that the data collected across an entire campus or even the health system is sufficient for general quality purposes, but due to the manner in which the data was aggregated, hospitals are unable to utilize the data to establish meaningful baselines.

Reliable data are key for successful dialogue between the hospital administration and physicians. Without validated data, oftentimes each side will bring their own information and unreliable anecdotes, and that can result in extremely slow progress. Early in CCMA development trust is key, and when each side asserts their own unverified claims regarding the current status of the service, trust can be lost between the parties.

For those reasons discussed earlier, hospitals that are considering a CCMA must evaluate the quality of their data sources and the quality of the tools available to the administration to efficiently and effectively gather concrete data. Validated baseline data are absolutely necessary to establish CCMA metrics.

Third-Party Valuation

Another critical component involving regulatory compliance and CCMAs involves fair market valuation. As mentioned previously, it is imperative that all base compensation contained within a CCMA is backed by a fair market value. In addition to being fair and reasonable commercially, CCMA fees also must

- Be set in place in advance by contract
- Not incentivize providers to withhold the care of Medicare and/or Medicaid beneficiaries
- Not reflect the volume nor the value of referrals received

Obtaining fair market value for the compensation that will be part of a CCMA is tricky though, due to the number of variables and the regulatory risk that each variable represents.

As such, an independent, third-party valuation must be obtained to determine the proper value of a CCMA. These third-party valuations are tailored for each specific CCMA, but are somewhat less objective than other valuation arrangements simply out of necessity due to the novel nature of each individual CCMA.

In the determination of a CCMA's fair market value, third-party firms use three approaches based on

1. Cost
2. Markets
3. Income

For the first of these approaches, the cost approach, valuation is determined on the basis of the number of hours that contracted physicians will work in providing both the base management services as well as meeting whatever performance measures and metrics that may be included as part of the CCMA. Once a particular range of hours that a physician will work has been established, a compensation package can be created using a fair market hourly rate given the individual physician's specialty and experience. But because the services provided as part of the base services are managerial and administrative, a physician's value is not necessarily equivalent to that of the physician's medical practice.

The last point is an important one. Fair market valuation of the physician's hourly wage does not correspond to a physician's lost opportunity cost of time spent away from their practice. Instead, this hourly rate is commensurate with that of what a physician would receive in the role of medical director or some other type of managerial role. For the sake of moving the negotiating process forward, it is crucial that this distinction is made and understood early in the process of CCMA formation. While there is a disparity between what a physician is paid hourly as an administrator and their lost opportunity cost of not practicing, this number does not reflect incentive compensation. With incentives, this disparity may be partially or completely erased, making the total compensation package much more attractive to prospective physicians. But there is more risk associated with this compensation arrangement, as incentives are dependent upon performance and corresponding metrics.

Of course, physicians across a multitude of specialties will be involved with CCMAs. How then will fair market valuation deal with differences in hourly rates across specialties keeping in mind the administrator and managerial roles served? There are a number of methods to address this concern and to fairly ensure that even though one specialty's physicians may make more than another, the rate determined for a CCMA will be fair. One of the most popular means by which to obtain this valuation is through what is called a blended hourly rate. The blended hourly rate simply takes the average hourly rate of a physician from each specialty, given their role as a medical director. So, regardless of which specialty a physician is contracted from to provide base services under a CCMA, the hourly rate will be the same under this blended hourly rate approach.

Another option includes distributing the base fee at a varying rate for differing specialties. This involves breaking a CCMA into different payment rates and grouping them by specialties depending on the fair market price of a given specialty. Consideration is then given to the hours that each of the differing specialties works as a part of the CCMA. This option is much riskier than the blended hourly rate approach though. As the base fee would be distributed by the physician-owned LLC, the hospital would not be able to effectively monitor fair market and regulatory criteria.

There is no comprehensive list of issues that affect fair market valuation. Any number of issues may arise during the creation of a CCMA that were not able to be foreseen before the process began. Instead of trying to provide a list of issues and solutions, there are six questions that guide fair market

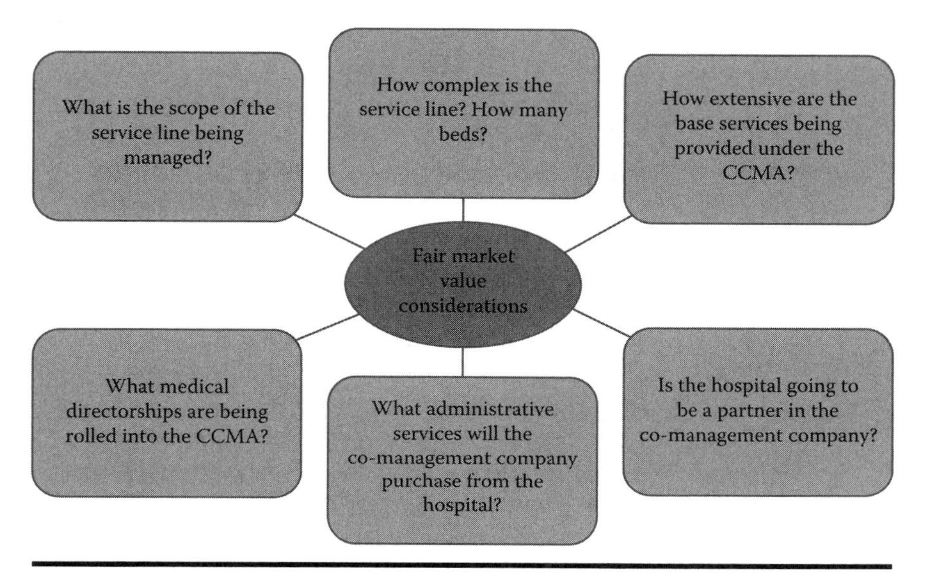

Figure 6.4 Fair market value considerations.

valuation (Figure 6.4). Throughout the valuation process, these questions should be kept in mind, issues should be evaluated against them, and consultations with third-party evaluators should serve as the final say in the manner.

The last issue relating to fair market valuation involves physicians' professional fees. Under most circumstances, preexisting reimbursement structures do not change as a result of enacting a CCMA. For instance, Medicare continues to reimburse hospitals based on PPS for inpatients and outpatients and physicians based on the Medicare Physician Fee Schedule. As long as a participating physician is not employed by the hospital, they will continue to collect all physician fee scheduled payments, but in addition to all management payments as part of an executed CCMA. If the physician is employed by the hospital or has some other professional services agreement in place prior to the CCMA, the physician would continue to report and assign their claims to the hospital under the same structure they maintained previously. They too would maintain their practice revenue while additionally increasing their total compensation with the added base and incentive fees coming as part of the CCMA.

Ongoing Performance Measure Development

Collecting data, establishing metrics, and developing effective performance measures are an ongoing process over the course of an executed CCMA. It is possible that some CCMAs do not include any of the aforementioned measures at its onset though. As such, these CCMAs would have no bonus structure, only the base management fees. This is common if data collection has not been established or it is not possible to establish reliable metrics. This is especially a concern when new facilities are open where data collection methods have not been established and where there is not already a body of data from which to draw from. Also, unique service lines do not lend themselves well to the creation of metrics and there may not be any regional or national benchmarks or any other accepted baseline from which performance measures can be established. In these cases, hospitals can still contract physicians in the development of service lines, as well as management and oversight. As facilities are established, data become more robust, or benchmarks become established, these limited CCMAs can and should be expanded.

Even without the need to expand beyond just management and oversight, CCMAs are a developing, iterative process. Performance measures are only as strong as the data that go into them. When that data is incomplete or inaccurate, physician performance is not being captured and consequently, patient care as well as incentive compensation may suffer. It is imperative that data be continually tracked and improved. This can be done in a number of ways including the following: improving upon collection methods, using physician guidance to better capture the data needed for a particular measure, or continual review of collected data to ensure data validity and that it accurately informs the specific performance measure.

As the collection of data improves over time, both with the improved coordination between physician needs and hospital expectations in addition to a more refined data collection process, the next step involves new metric development. While performance measure are identified and agreed upon as a part of the CCMA process, the metrics that assess that performance may need to be continually reviewed and developed further. Some service lines and procedures already have well-defined, medically accepted performance metrics and due to the nature of the service line or procedure, will not need the kind of resources devoted to development that others will need. Others though, like the more unique services lines mentioned previously, will need to incorporate new data as it becomes available into new metrics to effectively measure physician performance. Within the CCMA itself, when defining performance measures and their associated metrics, if the hospital and physician do not currently have the needed metric, the agreement can be written to allow the needed metrics to be included in the future. The development period as well as the expectations for hospital and physicians to work to establish those metrics can be written into the CCMA and once the metric has been created, can be added as an addendum. This process is essential in medicine as new techniques, procedures, and measurements need to continually be incorporated into CCMAs in order for performance measures to reflect each physician specialty's current best practices.

Conclusions

To summarize, entering into a CCMA requires careful consideration and planning to ensure proper development of supporting data and fair market value compensation. In terms of data, initial information to support benchmarks is essential.

This can take some additional time to implement. For compensation, base rates should be at fair market value, as should incentive compensation. Benchmarks triggering incentive compensation should be transparent and set in advance, for reasons discussed in the previous chapter. These payments should not affect normal reimbursement. In short, the hospital will still receive its facility payments, and the physicians will receive fees for professional services. Ensuring that these compensation schemes are carefully set out is necessary due to regulatory constraints, as was discussed in the preceding chapter.

Chapter 7

Clinical Co-Management Case Study

Introduction

Over the past several years, Murer Consultants, a legal-based healthcare management consulting firm, has had the opportunity to develop and implement Clinical Co-Management with numerous clients. What follows is a case study that seeks to amalgamate and synthesize our past experiences. Although the case study itself describes the ongoing development of a strategic regionalization plan for a tertiary medical system, nothing contained within can be attributed to any single client of Murer Consultants. All identifying characteristics of the institutions involved have been removed in order to preserve confidentiality. What remains are the most important aspects and issues of Clinical Co-Management development as identified by Murer Consultants, presented as a combined whole in the subsequent case study.

Case Study: Urban-Based Tertiary Medical System

A leading tertiary medical system (hereinafter referred to as the "Institution") retained Murer Consultants to assist in its long-term, multistate strategy to serve both urban and rural patient populations. The Institution desired to provide specialized tertiary care while partnering with community hospitals, health systems, and private physician groups in a multistate region. The Institution retained Murer Consultants to assist in designing the framework to partner with such regional healthcare institutions in order to accomplish this goal. Murer proposed, and the client agreed, to the utilization of Clinical Co-Management as the vehicle through which to achieve desired market share.

Initially, the Institution developed a partnership with a multihospital system focused on rural care (the "Hospital"). Under an executed Management Agreement, the Institution became the manager of the hospital's cardiology and orthopedic service lines. Also, as part of the agreement, the Institution would then subsequently engage a group of cardiologists and orthopedic surgeons in a co-management arrangement. The Clinical Co-Management Agreement (CCMA) would then act as the unification tool for the physicians from three parties—the tertiary medical center, the rural hospital's cardiology and orthopedic service lines, and nearby rural community cardiology and orthopedic practices—to collectively establish consistent protocols, policies, and procedures in order to reach an optimum level of compliance and quality, thereby effectively regionalizing the practice of cardiology and orthopedics in the region.

Murer Consultants developed the contractual framework, incorporating all elements necessary to comply with applicable fraud and abuse regulations, as described in Chapters 5 and 6. Under this framework, the Institution enters into a CCMA with the participating physicians via an established physician organization, which we will call Physician Co-Management Company, LLC. The base fee for management services provided to the physicians is paid by the Institution, as the Institution is responsible for the management of both the cardiology and orthopedic service lines via the management contract with the hospital. The incentive fee for achievement of performance standards by the physicians is paid by the hospital—the party that benefits most from the increased quality, efficiency, and cost savings—using the management contract as the vehicle for a relationship with the Physician Co-Management Company, LLC. Figure 7.1 illustrates these various agreements.

The aforementioned structure is complicated by the fact that two separate service lines are being contracted through the Physician Co-Management Company. In most circumstances, a CCMA will focus on an individual service line and will follow the guidelines put forth in Chapters 5 and 6. This structure though, with both cardiology and orthopedic surgery included, had to be organized in a somewhat different manner.

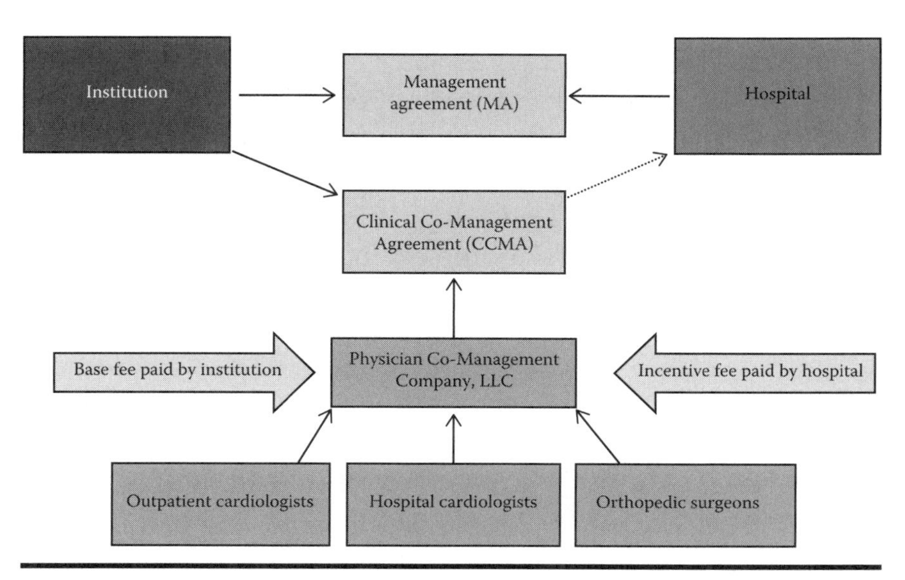

Figure 7.1 Agreement diagram.

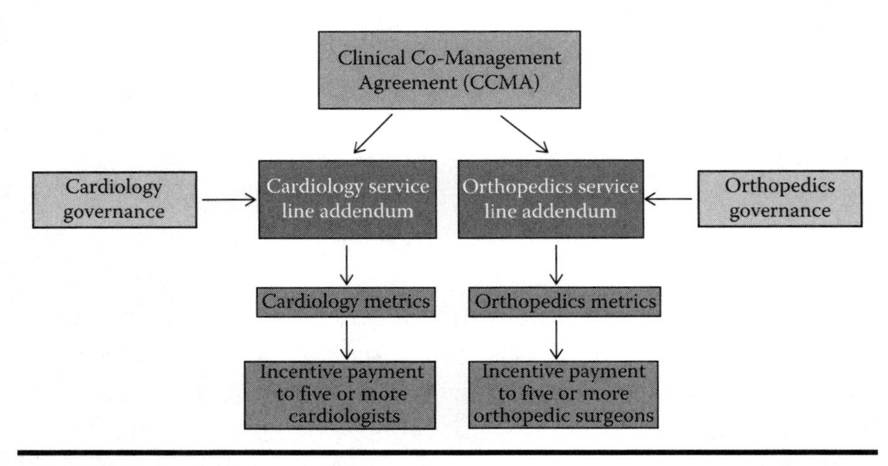

Figure 7.2 Service line addenda.

The CCMA is still the overarching agreement that integrates the Institution, Hospital, and Physician Co-Management Company, but each service line has its own specialty-specific addenda. In those addenda, metrics that involve at least five participating physicians were outlined and from those, the service line–specific per capita fee for physicians was determined (Figure 7.2). It is important to maintain these separate addenda in order to set up distinct governance of each service line and to provide the proper oversight required as per the regulations. Once that was established, the next step in the process involved the development of an implementation plan.

Working with senior leadership, Murer Consultants then developed an Action Plan to implement this framework. The plan set forth a step-by-step timeline for the completion of the Clinical Co-Management project and included the following:

- Identification of participants for and development of the Steering Committee
- Design of the CCMA goals via performance and quality metrics
- Assignment of management duties, including but not limited to the creation of protocols, policies, and procedures, to participating physicians

- Determination of CCMA base and incentive compensation via third-party valuation
- Implementation of CCMA governance via a Joint Council comprising at least one representative from all parties

The Steering Committee participants included a team member from Murer Consultants as the project leader, a senior Institution team member, a senior Hospital team member, and select administrators and physician leaders. A target "go live" date was set for 1 year after conception of the co-management agreement. This timeline allowed for a 1-year data collection process required for the establishment of performance and quality metric baselines, as described in Chapter 6. It is important to note that the processes related to the selection of performance and quality metrics and the planned year-long data collection and analysis helped to yield an increased understanding of the subject service line's operations and efficiency, as well as unification between administration and physicians working toward a common goal, results that are in themselves worth the efforts.

In order to begin these processes, the team led by Murer Consultants then designed and prioritized the goals of the Clinical Co-Management arrangement in terms of the clinical quality and efficiency criteria according to hospital performance and financial impact. The team selected quality metrics in eight categories that are as follows: (1) arrival, (2) discharge, (3) patient satisfaction, (4) mortality, (5) surgery, (6) inpatient orthopedic, (7) outpatient orthopedic, and (8) readmissions. National averages for the metrics from reputable data sources were researched and incorporated as benchmarks. The following scorecards were created, leaving the "baseline" column blank to be filled in once proper and validated data are collected: see Tables 7.1 through 7.8.

The 1-year data collection to complete this process is currently underway. Once completed, Murer Consultants will work with the Steering Committee to assess the baseline data

Table 7.1 Arrival Metrics

Arrival				
Metric	*Metric Source*	*Improvement*	*Baseline*	*Benchmark*
Median time from arrival to administration of fibrinolytic therapy in AMI patients with ST-segment elevation or left bundle branch block (LBBB) on the ECG performed closest to arrival time.	AMI-7	Decrease in median value		28 minutes
Median time from arrival to primary percutaneous coronary intervention (PCI) in AMI patients with ST-segment elevation or LBBB on the ECG performed closest to hospital arrival time.	AMI-8	Decrease in median value		<90 minutes
AMI patients who received aspirin within 24 h before or after hospital arrival.	AMI-1	Increase in percentage		96%

and benchmarks. Target goals will be determined, and ranges for the percentage-based incentive payments to the physicians will be established, in accordance with the methodology described in Chapters 5 and 6.

Specific management duties, such as the development and implementation of protocols, policies, and procedures, will

Table 7.2 Discharge Metrics

Discharge				
Metric	*Metric Source*	*Improvement*	*Baseline*	*Benchmark (%)*
Heart failure (HF) patients discharged home with written instructions or educational material given to patient or caregiver at discharge or during the hospital stay addressing *all* of the following: activity level, diet, discharge medication, follow-up appointment, weight monitoring, and what to do if symptoms worsen.	HF-1	Increase in percentage		94
HF patients with left ventricular systolic dysfunction (LVSD) who are prescribed an ACEI or ARB at hospital discharge.	HF-3	Increase in percentage		97

(*Continued*)

Table 7.2 (*Continued*) Discharge Metrics

Discharge				
Metric	*Metric Source*	*Improvement*	*Baseline*	*Benchmark (%)*
Surgery patients who were taking beta blockers before coming to the hospital, who were kept on the beta blockers during the period just before and after their surgery.	AMI-5	Increase in percentage		98
AMI patients who are prescribed a statin at hospital discharge.	AMI-10	Increase in percentage		98

Table 7.3 Patient Satisfaction Metrics

Patient Satisfaction				
Metric	*Metric Source*	*Improvement*	*Baseline*	*Benchmark*
Percentage of patients who reported that doctors "always" listened carefully to the patient and their family members during their hospital stay.	HCAHPS	Increase in percentage		82%

Table 7.4 Mortality Metrics

Mortality				
Metric	*Metric Source*	*Improvement*	*Baseline*	*Benchmark (%)*
Hospital 30-day mortality rate following heart failure (HF) hospitalization (Palliative Care Excluded).	MORT-30-HF	Decrease in percentage		12
CABG 30-day mortality rate.	STS	Decrease in percentage		3
Hospital 30-day mortality rate following acute myocardial infarction (AMI) hospitalization (palliative care excluded).	MORT-30-AMI	Decrease in percentage		15

then be designed and assigned to the participating physicians to enhance quality and efficiency of care as related to these metrics. For example, the Steering Committee will identify a concern on which to focus, that is proper utilization. Then, the Steering Committee will design a work plan targeted to this issue (Table 7.9).

Following consensus among all key stakeholders as to applicability of metric and targets and verification of baseline, the Institution will retain an independent valuation company to assess the proposed management duties as well as the target goals, thereby determining proper compensation to be paid to the physicians as a result of achieving performance targets. Each metric will be valued and a maximum aggregate

Table 7.5 Surgical Metrics

Surgical				
Metric	*Metric Source*	*Improvement*	*Baseline*	*Benchmark*
Routine pre-op antibiotic for cardiac operations—cefazolin and vancomycin (unless patient is allergic—then vancomycin or clindamycin and gentamycin).	SCIP guidelines	Increase in percentage		99%
Urinary catheter removal—removed on POD 1 or POD 2.	SCIP guidelines	Increase in percentage		97%
Return to OR for postoperative bleeding.	STS	Decrease in percentage		3%
Number of hours in ICU after cardiac surgery.	STS	Decrease in median value		24 h (72 if significant comorbidities present)

(*Continued*)

Table 7.5 (*Continued*) Surgical Metrics

Surgical				
Metric	*Metric Source*	*Improvement*	*Baseline*	*Benchmark*
Post-op renal failure.	STS	Decrease in percentage		≤30%
Percentage of patients seen within 72 h after consultation order is written during inpatient stay.	Murer/ internal	Increase in percentage		90%
Percentage of cases in which the attending physician signs off on procedure and equipment at time of scheduling when surgery is scheduled by a resident physician.	Murer/ internal	Increase in percentage		90%
Inpatient length of stay (LOS) in the hospital prior to elective surgery.	Murer/ internal	Decrease in days		1 day

(*Continued*)

Table 7.5 (*Continued*) Surgical Metrics

Surgical				
Metric	*Metric Source*	*Improvement*	*Baseline*	*Benchmark*
Length of time that lapses from the time a patient enters the OR to incision.	Murer/ internal	Decrease in minutes		20 minutes
Percentage of cases in which the attending physician changes the order of cases.	Murer/ internal	Decrease in percentage		15%
Period of time it takes to turnover/ prepare/set up an OR for a case/ procedure. Defined as wheels out (end time) and wheels in (start time of next case).	Murer/ internal	Decrease in time		30 minutes

(*Continued*)

Table 7.5 (*Continued*) Surgical Metrics

Surgical				
Metric	*Metric Source*	*Improvement*	*Baseline*	*Benchmark*
Percent of OR block time utilization by physicians measured by the specific block time through the block end time, allowing for average room turnover time (ortho) *Note:* Block time utilization is defined as a reservation of time and space.	Murer/ internal	Increase in utilization of block time		96%

(*Continued*)

Table 7.5 (*Continued*) Surgical Metrics

Surgical				
Metric	*Metric Source*	*Improvement*	*Baseline*	*Benchmark*
Percentage of first case of the day OR procedures that have on-time starts. Defined as the following: Patient in the Room; AND All instrumen-tation and equipment in the room; AND All personnel in the room as appropriate for the case; AND Attending physician signed off on procedure and equipment at time of scheduling surgery.	Murer/ internal	Increase in percentage		90%
Percentage of Day of Surgery Orthopedic Case Cancellations by physician for nonmedical reasons.	Murer/ internal	Decrease in rate		<2%

Table 7.6 Inpatient Orthopedic Metrics

Inpatient Orthopedic Unit				
Metric	*Metric Source*	*Improvement*	*Baseline*	*Benchmark*
Reduction in orthopedic inpatient cost per case, including Appropriate length of stay (LOS) and Appropriate use of resources.	Murer/ internal	Decrease in cost		$12,000
Prophylactic antibiotics discontinued within 24 h after surgery end time—hip	SCIP-3d	Increase in rate		99%–100%
Reduction in the number of readmissions to the acute hospital beds following an orthopedic inpatient stay. Readmission is defined as a readmission related to the most recent orthopedic inpatient admission.	Murer/ internal	Decrease in rate		<5%

(*Continued*)

Table 7.6 (*Continued*) Inpatient Orthopedic Metrics

Inpatient Orthopedic Unit				
Metric	*Metric Source*	*Improvement*	*Baseline*	*Benchmark*
Percentage of patients who reported that doctors "always" explained things in a way that the patient and their family members could understand.	HCAHPS	Increase in rate		93%

Table 7.7 Outpatient Orthopedic Clinic Metrics

Outpatient Orthopedic Clinic				
Metric	*Metric Source*	*Improvement*	*Baseline*	*Benchmark*
Percentage of patients who reported that doctors "always" explained things in a way that the patient and their family members could understand.	HCAHPS	Increase in rate		85%
Reduction in orthopedic outpatient clinic cost per visit	Murer/ internal	Decrease in cost		$57/visit

Table 7.8 Readmissions Metrics

Readmissions				
Metric	*Metric Source*	*Improvement*	*Baseline*	*Benchmark (%)*
Hospital 30-day readmission rate following heart failure (HF) hospitalization.	HF—30 day	Decrease in percentage		23
Hospital 30-day readmission rate following acute myocardial infarction (AMI) hospitalization.	AMI—30 day	Decrease in percentage		18
CABG 30-day readmission rate.	STS	Decrease in percentage		18

Table 7.9 Sample Clinical Co-Management Work Plan

Proper utilization
1. *Problem area*: Physicians are not meeting all of the regulatory requirements related to appropriate inpatient and outpatient utilization as related to observation conversions, 1-day stays, denials, readmits in 5 days, extended recovery time that has a significant impact on efficient patient care processes, costs and reimbursement.
2. *Potential objective*: Reduce the number of outliers related to appropriate inpatient utilization for patients.
3. *Sample factors that might contribute to meeting objective:* a. Lack of understanding of regulatory requirements. b. Surgeons not routinely following admission criteria. c. Lack of coordination/communication with nursing and case management. d. Institutional delays related to particular services.
4. *How co-management company may help achieve objective:* a. Participate in Case Management meetings to improve understanding of reasons for inappropriate utilization and effect changes in surgeons behaviors. b. Develop protocols working with Case Management to improve physician practices to include algorithms to avoid need to call physicians and developing list of diagnoses that would require a call to the physician. c. Provide regular educational opportunities for physicians to learn how to avoid inappropriate utilization. d. Work with hospital to implement process changes to avoid institutionally caused delays in care. e. Educate clinical Associates on processes to help reduce practices leading to inappropriate utilization.

payment to the participating physicians will be determined. Finally, at least 90 days prior to the expiration of each year throughout the term of the agreement, the Steering Committee will review the data and "re-base" the quality metrics baselines and incentive-based compensation as well as the management duties and base fee compensation, in accordance with the method described in Chapters 5 and 6.

Chapter 8

Conclusion and Next Steps

Clinical Co-Management is a story without an ending. Once put into place, a Clinical Co-Management Agreement (CCMA) is continually evolving, with performance, metrics, and goals being reevaluated, redefined, and reaffirmed on an annual basis. If one of the goals of healthcare is to continually improve upon the process and delivery of medicine, including increasing quality and efficiency, evaluation must likewise evolve. Through Clinical Co-Management, guidelines are established, working relationships are fostered, care is improved by constantly monitoring performance quality, and incentives are paid accordingly, but the agreement is purposely left open-ended in order to be responsive to the needs of the parties involved, advances in the field of medicine, and to the patients themselves.

The Conclusion Is That There Is No Conclusion

For Clinical Co-Management to have a beneficial effect on the effective delivery of healthcare, we must recognize a number of factors going forward. First among these is the realization that Clinical Co-Management challenges the historical paradigm of healthcare in the United States. Hospitals are not used to abdicating components of control and management of their service lines to outside entities. Likewise, physicians are not used to putting such an emphasis on administrative and managerial roles nor has their compensation been tied so directly to performance and outcomes. It is easy to recognize the potential benefits offered through adopting Clinical Co-Management, but changing the direction of a ship as large and complicated as healthcare, one that is charged with politics and social mores, is a difficult proposition to say the least.

Additionally, there is a real struggle between the day-to-day reality of a fragmented healthcare system and the desire for better integrated and coordinated care across specialties and venues of care. Something as basic as finding common language between departments or defining a cost-per-case that is agreed upon by hospital administrators and physicians presents formidable barriers to alleviating this struggle. Without a common starting point or an agreed-upon methodology from which both parties can confidently enter into a working relationship, the system will remain fragmented, quality of care will suffer, and gains in efficiency will not be realized.

The Value Is in the Process

The process of entering into a CCMA serves as the beginning point moving from fragmentation to coordination. Where there was no common language between departments or hospitals or disparate venues of care, Clinical Co-Management serves to eliminate dialects through the arduous process of forging a new, holistic identity. This new identity focuses on the patient as a whole and his or her movement within and interaction with the healthcare system. Gone are the days of the production line mind-set, where each specialty and department and facility are fully compartmentalized, responsible for one part of the patient, without respect given to the final product. A change of mind-set and a change of imagination are as required as changing the method of payment delivery to effect real and substantial change in this regard.

The work only really begins once the CCMA is signed. This marks the beginning of an iterative process in which hospitals and physicians go back and forth and in many respects find that common language for the first time. During this period, the respective parties test and validate the accuracy of each other's assumptions through data. From this point, trust is built, costs can be determined, and worthwhile metrics can finally be agreed upon. It is also a long-term process that requires at least 3 years to determine the functionality and to overcome the obstacles associated with new CCMAs.

The Perils of Clinical Co-Management Valuation

As discussed in Chapter 6, the valuation of a CCMA is a critical step in ensuring compliance with federal regulatory statutes and is a service that few firms provide currently. It is important to recognize and understand what is included within these third-party evaluations as many of these firms, while financially adept, have little experience with CCMAs themselves or in navigating the complex regulatory environment that surrounds Clinical Co-Management. Beware of any valuation that

- Determines the base fee without taking physician's specialty into account
- Fails to explicitly identify or individually weighs performance metrics
- Lacks a mechanism that ties incentive compensation to performance metrics

- Incentivizes physicians to maintain status quo performance
- Appears to produce an unreasonable fair market rate given the specialty and expected duties and hours worked

Once these initial pitfalls are overcome, the real source of strength of Clinical Co-Management comes from the Joint Councils, in which a platform for the exchange of information is created between hospitals and physicians. As this is at least a 3-year process, these councils serve as forums to rewrite the rules of engagement between historical contentious and suspicious demeanors and instead offer a nondefensive, nonaccusatory medium for solving problems based on validated trust. All issues that arise should not be reacted to in an emergency manner. Instead, issues should be aggregated and meetings should be had that then turn the collective hospital administrator–physician group to problem solvers instead of simply problem identifiers.

The future is bright indeed for Clinical Co-Management. Few alternative payment and delivery mechanisms offer both the data-backed, concrete levels of verifiable trust between parties and the flexibility to annually reevaluate performance, goals, and direction like Clinical Co-Management can and has done time and time again. As pressure continues to mount and the financial realities of healthcare continue to move further and further away from traditional models, it is important to examine what feasible and realistic changes can be made to improve competitiveness and to position oneself better as the healthcare environment continues to evolve. Clinical Co-Management not only serves as the short-term answer to integrate services but to bridge historically separated groups within the healthcare system, it also positions one well for the long term, laying the foundation and creating the common language needed for the bundled payment delivery mechanisms of the future.

Index

J

M

O

P